AMERICAN COLONIAL

WENDELL GARRETT

AMERICAN COLONIAL

PURITAN SIMPLICITY
TO
GEORGIAN GRACE

EDITED AND DESIGNED BY DAVID LARKIN

PRINCIPAL PHOTOGRAPHY BY PAUL ROCHELEAU

THE MONACELLI PRESS
A DAVID LARKIN BOOK

For my daughter Abigail
"There is but one virtue, justice,
one duty, to be happy."
—Denis Diderot,
Eléments de Physiologie, 1774–80

First published in the United States of America in 1995 by
The Monacelli Press, Inc.,
10 East 92nd Street, New York, New York 10128

Library of Congress Catalog Card Number: 95-75838
ISBN: 1-885254-99-7

Monacelli Press Editor: David Brown
Design Production: Meredith Miller

Printed and bound in Italy

Half title: Polished-iron-and-brass candlestick
of about 1750 from Germany or Switzerland
Frontispiece: Walnut child's chair of about 1750
from Ephrata Cloister, Ephrata, Pennsylvania

CONTENTS

NEW ENGLAND TAKES SHAPE

England's Discovery of America:

Earth's Only Paradise

The world known to Englishmen in 1485—the year Henry VII came to the throne—was small and cramped. To the simple farmer the world was limited to his village, its surrounding fields, and the nearest market town. To the merchants and mariners in the West Country of England, who did business over the Atlantic's great waters and enjoyed a prosperous trade with Iceland and the Azores, the world was larger but still confined to their trade routes.

England had long been an intellectual and economic backwater, far outstripped in importance and wealth by the great Italian city-states. Indeed, Henry VII, first of the House of Tudor, was offered Columbus's enterprise but turned it down. The Mediterranean was the vital center of trade and commerce, learning and exploration, art and literature. The widening of human horizons began there with the Renaissance and was carried outward by the scholars and seafarers of Europe's southern coast. Knowledge of a wider world that included Columbus's discoveries seeped slowly into England, trickling down from the men of the court, counting house, and deep-sea wharf to an ever-broader circle in London, eventually to country houses, and ultimately to the common farmers and craftsmen who would become colonists.

The Americas caught the imagination of Englishmen in the late sixteenth and early seventeenth centuries. By the time of Elizabeth's death in 1603, America seemed an easy land where riches of every sort could be had with little effort. The new territories appeared in plays, pamphlets, and poems and, more importantly, were continually talked about, as facts and fancies were passed by word of mouth.

Englishmen first saw the New World through Spanish eyes: the New World was the Caribbean and New Spain, a warm and languid land, rich in tropical fruits and, of course, gold and silver. Playwright George Chapman, in *Eastward Hoe* (1605), had one character exclaim in vigorous Elizabethan English: "Come, boys, Virginia longs till we share the rest of her maidenhead . . . I tell

thee, gold is more plentiful there than copper is with us . . . Why, man, all their dripping-pans and their chamber-pots are pure gold; and all the chains with which they chain up their streets are massy gold; all the prisoners they take are fettered in gold; and for rubies and diamonds, they go forth on holidays and gather them by the seashore." Gold and gems would remain a part of the imagery of America. As late as 1619, in his ode *The Virginian Voyage*, Michael Drayton would send Britons forth "to get the pearl and gold, and ours to hold, Virginia, earth's only paradise."

In Sir Thomas More's *Utopia* (1516), perfection and riches were combined, and the New World seemed to promise the fulfillment of More's ideal. By some subtle alchemy the lush riches and idyllic, Eden-like qualities of the Americas would transform sloth to diligence and vice to virtue; the trollop would find chastity, the fop industry, the ostentatious frugality. The New World could be an attempt to draw anew and more perfectly the outlines of human society. The image of America as an easy, gold-rich land promising opportunity would continue to tantalize Englishmen, and it underlay the beginnings of English colonization.

English America was, in reality, neither a rich nor an easy land. Those who sailed to settle Virginia and New England with that image in mind were doomed to disappointment. The first decade of English colonies in the Western Hemisphere was experimental, singularly unsuccessful, and miserable indeed. Colonists died of disease and starvation and, having antagonized the local Indians within weeks of their arrival, of arrows as well. In an almost frantic search for something of value which could be produced and shipped home, the first colonists tried a string of different commodities—wine, glass, iron, silk—until the value of tobacco, the "Indian weed," was discovered. Virginia went tobacco-mad and its cultivation formed the economic basis of the first successful English colonies in North America. Virginia tobacco created an English market, despite smoking's ill repute (in 1604

King James I pronounced smoking to be "loathsome to the eye, hatefull to the Nose, harmfull to the brain, [and] dangerous to the Lungs"). However, it was good for tax rolls, and by the 1630s tobacco was firmly established as Virginia's staple crop and chief source of revenue.

England's continental colonies, those that would eventually rebel and form the United States, were laid down over the course of the next century. Following the settlement of Jamestown in 1607, Plymouth was begun in New England in 1620. Its origins lay in a small group of English religious dissenters, known as Separatists, who condemned the English church as utterly sinful and broke with both it and their country to establish their own reformed and separate church. These religiously disconsolate Puritans set sail from Plymouth, England, in September 1620 aboard the crowded *Mayflower* and landed in America two months later, farther north than they had intended. There, on a fine harbor, they established their colony and named it after the city from which they had sailed. Before the Pilgrims landed, their leaders drew up the famous Mayflower Compact, which almost all the adult men signed, wherein they formed a "civil body politic" and promised "all due submission and obedience" to such "just and equal laws" as the government they set up might pass.

In England, meanwhile, conditions were rapidly deteriorating. The melancholia faintly sensed in Elizabeth's reign became more apparent with each year of the reigns of her Stuart successors, James I and Charles I. In asserting royal prerogatives, the Stuarts riled the English gentry and the Parliament which they dominated. In part, the malaise was associated with religion; the Stuart kings seemed far too tolerant of Catholicism in England. There was also general alarm over the dramatic social and economic changes caused by the doubling of the English population over the previous 150-year period. In these new, unprecedented demographics, Englishmen with sizable land holdings could substantially improve their lot. Others, particularly landless laborers and those with very small amounts of land, fell into unremitting poverty. The streets and highways were filled with steady streams of the landless and homeless, and the population of cities, especially London, swelled. Many believed that England was overcrowded; they easily concluded that colonies in the New World could siphon off England's "surplus population," relieving social strains at home.

Many others decided that they could improve their own conditions by migrating from their small, land-scarce, overpopulated island to a large, land-rich continent. Such economic considerations affected the decision to migrate to the colonies as much, if not more than, a desire to escape from religious persecution. The great migration of 1620–42 was thus the result of extraordinary dislocations in English society, a swarming of the "great and superfluous multitude," which caused men and women to seek an escape to the New World.

The Morning of New England:
An Errand Into the Wilderness

The progress of the Plymouth colony was steady rather than spectacular. William Bradford, a thirty-year-old farmer of simple genius, was elected governor after the first one died, and his firm but fair rule brought him the confidence of the majority. Around 1630, Bradford began to write *The History of Plymouth Plantation*, a great hymn that captures the sweep and majesty of the Pilgrim experience. Looking back, he chanted about the landfall in one of the great passages in New England literature: "May not and ought not the children of these fathers rightly say: Our fathers were Englishmen which came over this great ocean, and were ready to perish in this wilderness; but they cried unto the Lord, and he heard their voyce, and looked on their adversitie." The arrival of the Pilgrims in Plymouth was, in retrospect, a turning point in English colonization, for it marked the beginning of a voluntary movement to America, a movement that would swell to a flood by the 1630s.

Before the end of the 1620s, another group of Puritans—this time Congregationalists, not Separatists—launched the colonial enterprise that would come to dominate New England, the Massachusetts Bay Company. These Congregationalists were Puritans of the "middling sort"; not driven out of England, they came to the New World of their own accord. They were artisans, tradesmen, and yeomen with a sense of mission, sent on "an errand into the wilderness." They spoke as fully as they knew how, and none more magnificently or cogently than John Winthrop, a pious but practical Suffolk landowner. Aboard the ship *Arbella*, in the midst of the passage, he delivered a lay sermon, "A Modell of Christian Charity," laying out his expectations for the new colony. Above all, he stressed the communal nature of their endeavor, their belief that God had disposed humankind in a hierarchy of social classes, so that "in all times some must be rich, some poore, some highe and eminent in power and dignitie; others meane and in subjeccion." But differences in status did not imply differences in worth. On the contrary, in Winthrop's simple but splendid words, God had planned the world so that "every man might have need of other, and from hence they might be all knitt more nearly together in the Bond of brotherly affection." In America, the Massachusetts Bay Company was performing a job not so much for God as for history, Winthrop asserted. More was at stake than just one little colony, "for wee must Consider that wee shall be as a Citty upon a Hill, the Eies of all people are uppon us."

Under ordinary circumstances, the kind of community Winthrop described would have been rooted in a particular soil and linked by ties of family, church, government, and ancient custom. By these standards, the Puritan community established in Massachusetts in 1630 was quite heterogeneous. While most of the settlers were English, and many were Puritan, they had all been uprooted, and they lacked the ordinary and expected common ties. This was a new community on new land, with a new church not yet firmly established and with a government of questionable legal force. What Winthrop counted on to hold this body together was an extraordinary outpouring of Christian love, an outpouring that came from the idea that they were a chosen people with a mission.

The Puritans' communal ideal was expressed chiefly in the doctrine of the covenant—they believed God had made a covenant, an agreement or contract, with them when he chose them for their mission to America. In turn they covenanted with each other, promising to work together toward their goals. The Massachusetts Bay colony's method of distributing land also helped further the communal ideal. The early settlers, transplanted Englishmen from manorial, village, or town communities, tended to reestablish traditional farming practices and familiar town plans in New England. In Massachusetts, groups of families—often from the same region of England—applied together to the General Court for grants of land on which to establish towns. In the center of the town, dwellings were generally constructed on "house lots" of less

than an acre. Outside this central grouping lay open fields divided into individual lots, some for plowlands and farming, others for meadowlands and grazing, and others were marsh and woodland. Common lands were also set aside for general use. This nuclear village/open field system stands in sharp contrast to the more dispersed farms and plantations of Virginia and the later southern colonies.

The New England Town:
Continued Toyl of Erecting Houses

The church—usually the Congregational church—was the nucleus of the early New England towns, many of which were settled by a minister and his flock. Every town was required to have a minister, and the people in it were obliged to pay his salary and attend his church whether they were members or not. The church meetinghouse stood on its own plot, typically the town green or some higher ground within easy reach of each house. The location was central by necessity, for the meetinghouse served not only as a house of worship but also as a community center and the seat of town government. The building itself was of no preordained style, but in keeping with Puritan austerity, simplicity and modesty were its hallmarks. No great cathedrals or spired stone churches rose on New England soil; instead, rough, square, wooden structures were common, usually capped by four-planed pyramidal roofs and modest bell cupolas.

In its classic form, the economic life of the New England village was made up of farmers with all the skills needed to maintain the community. Every townsman was given ample land to support himself, and though there were traces of deference to rank, there was also an abundance of land and a policy that each man would have enough to survive and even prosper. Extremes of wealth and poverty were deliberately avoided. In time, however, the jack-of-all-trades gave way to men with specialized skills and trades, and the concentration of these men came to mark off the town from the surrounding farms. Town industry in these years consisted of such small-scale ventures as tanning, cabinetmaking, shoemaking, and plow and barrel-stave manufacturing—enterprises designed both to meet the needs of the town and the adjacent farms and to provide a surplus for export to the nearest coastal city. Although such undertakings by independent artisans are often seen as the golden age of the small-town economy, these enterprises were highly precarious and extremely transitory. The tradition-bound colonial craftsman was defenseless against minor shifts in the economic pattern; with little capacity to adapt to changing demands, no efficient marketing channels, little or no capital, and few credit resources, many failed or changed occupations with monotonous regularity. Some New England colonial towns struggled to maintain some degree of stability by passing statutes that regulated wages and prices, but rising competition and a chronic labor shortage made these measures difficult to implement.

The most familiar aspect of small-town political life is undoubtedly the New England town meeting. It was, in essence, the church congregation assembled to decide secular matters. At the earliest meetings voting was confined to freemen, a status determined by property and church membership, but this practice soon deteriorated, as it was simply not feasible to govern with a minority. Eventually only minors, women, tenants, and persons who had not been accepted as inhabitants were excluded. The meetings were presided over by a moderator, whose main responsibility was the reconciliation of conflicting viewpoints. The town's executive arm was made up of the selectmen—chosen by election and usually seven in number—the secular equivalent of the church's elders (as prescribed in Proverbs 9:1, "Wisdom hath builded her house, she hath hewn out her seven pillars"). The town meeting became the decision-making body: it imposed taxes, determined how much each man would pay, spent town money, authorized land divisions, settled title disputes, approved new immigrants as inhabitants, arranged for fencing common land and settled the endless disputes over common-land use, located highways, arranged for animal pounds, granted economic concessions to exploit various local resources, and gave permission to engage in various kinds of business.

There was no line drawn between God's province and that of the world. Everything one did and thought—one's craft, one's crops, one's family life—were under the direct eye and constant superintendence of the Almighty. The church was made up of "visible saints," people who had met vigorous spiritual and worldly requirements and demonstrated that they led exemplary Christian lives. But the flesh was lamentably weak; in the souls of even the stoutest of saints the warfare between God and the Devil was unremitting. The ways in which sinners might fall were many: malicious gossip, sinful anger, extreme intemperance, falsehoods, abuse of wives by husbands and of husbands by wives, flagrant neglect of family worship, betting on horse racing, dishonest business dealings, desecration of the Sabbath, profanity, propagation of scandal, incest, lewd behavior, and murder. Two of the most frequent breaches of church discipline were fornication and adultery. As early as 1668 the General Court of Massachusetts had deplored the large number of bastards in the colony, and the church records of all New England towns contain the confessions of many married couples who had had sexual relations before marriage. The general rule of the time was that any child born less than seven months after the marriage of its parents was presumed to have been conceived out of wedlock, and the parents were expected to confess and to express their penitence. But as long as sexual activity outside of marriage culminated in wedlock and the production of offspring, or did not destroy the unity of the family, it was regarded with astonishing tolerance. Congregations were doubtless on occasion cruel, but within a harsh, authoritarian system the records provide impressive evidence that most showed great patience and forbearance with the sinners who appeared before them. Two examples show the range of both crime and punishment: Ebenezer Parker of Cambridge, Massachusetts, had tried to stab his wife but, upon public confession, was restored to full communion in his church. However, a man accused of deliberately singing off-key in order to interfere with orderly worship was excommunicated for impenitence.

The Thomas Lee house, East Lyme, Connecticut, built about 1660. The original portion of the house is the left half of the present structure.

The Timber-Framed Houses of New England:
All Things to Do

Colonization along the Atlantic seaboard was the process of building not just governments and societies but also homes and farms where before there was nothing. New England was a "howling desart," wrote Edward Johnson in *Wonder-Working Providence*, where "the onely encouragements were the laborious breaking up of bushy ground, with the continued toyl of erecting houses." Colonists throughout the New World had "all things to do, as in the beginning of the world," as one wrote. The first colonists in Massachusetts were mainly English men and women who had lived in small agricultural communities, for the most part rudely educated, simple people—small farmers, artisans, and petite bourgeoisie from the towns of East Anglia and the southwestern counties. The first generation of immigrants brought with them the building practices and traditions of postmedieval vernacular English architecture.

The lives and attitudes of the first colonists must be seen as part of a continuum; once transplanted to the Western Hemisphere, they never wholly ceased to be English, and there is thus a close relationship between the buildings in which the emigrants had grown up and those they erected upon their arrival in New England. The only building art they had known firsthand was the modest vernacular house of oak timber frame and a two-room (hall/parlor), central-chimney plan, and it was this style that became the preferred one in the New World.

Oak was the traditional building material. The timbers, once felled, were shaped with an ax and trimmed with an adze or sawn with a pit saw. The massive elements of the house frame were held together by mortise-and-tenon joints; tenons were cut with a hand saw, mortises were made with an auger and squared with a mallet and a chisel, and dowel holes were bored with the auger. The timbers, used soon after they were felled, were allowed to dry in place, as the splits and checks commonly found in the larger timbers of oak well attest. The heavy frame, once assembled and prepared, was raised into place under the direction of the joiners and carpenters according to a carefully considered pattern and sequence of erection. The frame was then stiffened by angle braces at the corners and by heavy beams, called chimney girts, which ran across the length of the house, abutting the chimney on either side. From the chimney girts to the main girts on either end of the house ran another huge structural member, the summer bean. Within this massive, boxlike frame were the lighter vertical studs of the walls and the horizontal joists that supported the floors. For insulation, the wall spaces between the studs were filled with wattle and daub (a close network of sticks or riven staves plastered with a mixture of clay or lime) or with rough brick masonry known as nogging—both originally English techniques. The entire structure was protected on the outside by white pine clapboards. The roof consisted of pairs of common rafters, joined and pegged together at their apex without a ridge piece, and braced by a collar beam about a third of the way down their length. The elaborate roof-framing system of timbers—collar purlins, crown posts, and tie beams—imparted longitudinal stability to the frame. The insertion of the massive central chimney stack also added to the structural stability.

Among the more striking features of the New England house were the two-story enclosed porch, the facade gables, and the projection of one story over another (at the time called a jetty but now known as an overhang). The jetty was a traditional English feature that persisted throughout the seventeenth century in both the Old World and the New, and in its hewn form can be found in New England as late as the early nineteenth century. The origins of jettied houses have been much debated, the prevalent myth being that where building space was limited in crowded English and continental cities, projecting, cantilevered upper stories provided larger rooms, although they darkened streets below. More plausible structural reasons for the jetty have also been advanced, suggesting that shorter posts were easier to obtain than long timbers, and carpenters recognized that the frame of a house could be strengthened with projecting stories. The jetty provided two places instead of one to make the necessary joints for the junctions of the vertical posts with the horizontal girts. But the supply of

timber was diminishing rapidly, particularly for good oak, and it became necessary to build on simpler lines. Robert Reyce, writing in Suffolk in 1603, observed that "the carelesse wast . . . of our wonted plenty of timber, and other building stuffe, hath enforced the witt of this latter age to devise a new kind of compacting, uniting, coupling, framing, and building, with almost half the timber which was wont to bee used, and far stronger."

The preferred seventeenth-century house plan was that of two rooms, one usually a little larger than the other, on either side of a central chimney. Often there would be a lean-to at the rear, and sometimes the small entry was projected to provide a two-story enclosed porch. The two principal ground-floor rooms were called the parlor or best room and the hall or keeping room. The rooms above them were called the parlor chamber and the hall chamber, and the main room in the lean-to was the kitchen. To one side of the kitchen, usually at the cooler end, was a buttery or dairy.

The living habits of New Englanders were thoroughly in keeping with trends in old England. The seventeenth-century parlor had multiple uses, all related to its character as the best room: here was the best furniture, here company was dined and entertained, and here slept the parents of the house. William Bentley, the Salem diarist, noted in 1812 that during the seventeenth century, "no families or heads of families lodged on the second stories." Indeed, the ground-floor parlor remained the master bedroom well into the eighteenth and in some cases even into the nineteenth century. There was always a table in the parlor, and while there were virtually no floor coverings at the time, carpets were placed on the table. The hall was an all-purpose living and cooking area, where the many cooking utensils and fireplace equipment used in the preparation and consumption of food were found. In addition to chairs, tables, boxes, chests, and cupboards, there was apt to be a bed in the hall (of less value than the parents'), a settle (wooden bench), and often some tools and light farm equipment. Upper chambers were normally given over to bedding and storage of barrels, skins, grain, provisions, yarn, spinning and weaving equipment, and "lumber," an archaic term for odds and ends. Inventories of furnishings from simpler houses make it clear that the upper rooms were often set up in dormitory fashion, with more than one bed in each chamber. They were also used for the storage of miscellaneous staples and foodstuffs.

During the early years of the eighteenth century, a four-room plan with central passage spread widely as an expression of the new academic style, in which functionalism was exchanged for an expansive formality. With higher ceilings and larger windows, the rooms themselves acquired a new sense of spaciousness, and structural elements that had been exposed in the seventeenth century were now almost entirely masked with plaster and finely molded trim. Dignified by a broad paneled staircase, the small entry area was now called the great entry. Of the four principal rooms on the ground floor, at least two served as parlors—the best parlor was reserved for the best affairs, and the second, or common, parlor designed for less formal uses. The two remaining principal rooms on the ground floor were the hall or keeping room and the kitchen. The keeping room was the ancestor of the modern living room and combined the functions of living, dining, and occasionally, sleeping. The kitchen was almost always located in the lean-to at the rear of the house, or in the cellar.

Even the simplest houses at Massachusetts Bay were carpenter-built—colonists did not build their own houses, so the trained carpenter's skill was essential. Francis Higginson of Salem wrote home to friends in 1629: "Of all trades, carpenters are most needful; therefore bring as many as you can." The New England economy was too primitive to support substantial vocational specialization, but carpenters were an exception. Promotional literature such as William Wood's in 1634 sought to recruit carpenters. Among the men who would be "most fit for these plantations," he specifies "an ingenious Carpenter, a cunning Joyner . . . and a good brick-maker, a Tyler and a Smith." Any person with skill in these trades, he continues, "needs not feare but he may improve his time and endeavors to his owne benefit." This shortage of craftsmen was perennial; in 1752 an advertisement of Robert Waller of Norfolk, Virginia, announced that he was "much in Want of House-Joiners."

A great proportion of the early American carpenters came from small villages or rural communities where, traditionally, the young builder was apprenticed to an established master-workman for a seven-year period that spanned most of his teen years. During the earliest years of settlement most incoming carpenters at Massachusetts Bay gave their age as twenty-one or twenty-two, apparently having already completed their apprenticeships. Later,

in 1660, owing to the unsuccessful adaptation of the traditional apprenticeship system, a Boston selectman complained that "many youthes in this Towne, being put forth Apprentices to severall manufactures and sciences, but for 3 or 4 yeares time, contrary to the Customes of all well governed places," had not unexpectedly become "uncapable of being Artists in their trades." More important, they had revealed an "unmeetnes" at the expiration of their term "to take charge of others for government and manuall instruction in their occupations." It was ordered "that no person shall henceforth open a shop in this Towne, nor occupy any manufacture or science, till hee hath compleated 21 years of age, nor except hee hath served seven yeares Apprentice-ship."

In the New World, where there were no preexisting dwellings that could be repaired or enlarged, the volume of new building was astonishing, and carpenters enjoyed the financial rewards of great demand. By November 1633, Massachusetts Bay Governor Winthrop was complaining that "the scarcity of workmen had caused them to raise their wages to an excessive rate, so as a carpenter would have three shillings the day, a laborer two shillings and sixpence, etc." Records show that steps were taken again and again to regulate wages, without lasting effect.

The earliest English carpenters brought not only their knowledge of the trade but also their familiar building tools. Francis Higginson, writing to England in 1629, before the mass migration had begun, urged prospective emigrants to "be sure to furnish yourselves with things fitting to be had, before you come . . . all manner of carpenters' tools, and a good deal of iron and steel to make nails, and locks for houses . . . and glasses for windows, and many other things, which were better for you to think of them there than to want them here." William Wood, also concerned with advising prospective settlers, urged them in 1634 to bring "all manner of tooles for Workmen . . . with Axes both broad and pitching axes. All manner of Augers, piercing bits, Whip-saws, Two-handed saws, Froes, both for the riving of Pailes and Laths, rings for Beetles heads, and Iron-wedges."

Although tools had to be imported, raw materials did not. A number of contemporary accounts mention the abundant supplies found in the virgin forests of North America. In 1634 William Wood assured the prospective planter that "the Timber of the Countrey growes straight, and tall, some trees being twenty, some thirty foot high, before they spread forth their branches . . . The chiefe and common Timber for ordinary use is Oake, and Walnut. Of Oakes there be three kindes, the red Oake, white, and blacke; as these are different in kinde, so are they chosen for such uses as they are most fit for, one kind being more fit for clappboard, others for sawne board, some fitter for shipping, others for houses." Furniture makers preferred the red oak with its greater porosity and knot-free expanse of trunk, while white oak, more resistant to rot, was popular for house frames. John Evelyn reported to the Royal Society in 1662 that the "Chestnut is (next to the Oak) one of the most sought after by the Carpenter and Joyner." In 1663 John Jossel wrote of the white cedar that "this Tree the English [at Massachusetts Bay] saw into boards to floor their Rooms, for which purpose it is excellent, long lasting, and wears very smooth and white; likewise they make shingles to cover their houses with instead of tyle, it will never warp." William Wood wrote of the ubiquitous New England pine, "The Firre and Pine bee trees that grow in many places, shooting up exceeding high, especially the Pine. They doe afford good masts, good board, Rozin and Turpentine." The almost exclusive use of pine for finish trim, including doors, window sashes, partitions, and floors is overwhelmingly demonstrated in the seventeenth-century houses of Massachusetts.

The first settlers at Massachusetts Bay left England at a time when timber depletion was becoming a widespread problem, and in spite of what must have seemed like inexhaustible forest reserves, the colonists moved quickly to regulate the supply. Throughout the century, New England towns ordered the conservation of local timber resources. As early as 1637, the town of Salem ordered "that henceforward noe sawyer clapboard cleaver or any other person whatsoever shall cutt down saw or cleave any boards or tymber within our lymits and transport them to other places." The recorder explained, "we have found by experience that the transporting of boards and clapboards from our plantation hath . . . bared our woods verie much of the best tymber trees of all sorts." The town of Dedham in 1667 focused on the necessity of rationing its richly wooded hinterland; the selectmen observed "that great waste is made in the wood and timber in the Common Lande of the Towne," and this they judged "very prejudiciall at present but especially for the succeeding generations which it concerne us to consider."

Seventeenth-Century Woodworking Craftsmen and Their Joinery:

Art and Mysterie

The religious scruples of the Puritan settlers did not preclude them from enjoying material prosperity and visual delight, and for their furniture they preferred the extravagant late-medieval designs and forms of mannerism. First a style of painting, mannerism began in Italy in the early sixteenth century and is characterized by exaggerated proportions and spatial incongruity. Furniture soon manifested this new fashion, and grotesque ornament and exotic motifs became accepted parts of the decorative vocabulary. After the invasion of the Netherlands by the Spanish in 1572, many extremely able Dutch and North German craftsmen of Protestant convictions fled to England and brought with them a broad, practical knowledge of mannerist forms and decoration. In the late sixteenth century, during the stable reign of Elizabeth I, mannerism became the newest fashion and a badge of Protestant solidarity. It is not surprising, then, that the Puritans who left for New England in the 1620s and 1630s were comfortable with and proficient in mannerist forms and decoration; indeed, it formed part of their identity as Englishmen.

Furniture in New England was made first by joiners and turners, and later by cabinetmakers. The techniques a seventeenth-century carpenter used to frame a house are similar to those used by a joiner to frame a table or a piece of case furniture. A square or rectangular wood frame was made, held together by mortise-and-tenon joints and fastened with wooden pins. These frames could be grooved on their inner perimeters, and feather-edged boards were fitted into the grooves to form panels for the heads of beds, backs of chairs, and wainscot walls. Although the joiner's framing technique was a scaled-down and simplified version of that of the house carpenter, the joiner had more and smaller tools to produce work of more intricate detail and finer scale. Joined work was usually embellished with planed molding of decorative grooves and "linen-fold" carving, which looked like textile hangings. Carving was the most common decorative technique used by the early joiners of rural New England. Their abstract floral carving, which is found on the most ambitious seventeenth-century New England furniture, was laid out with a rule, a square, a pair of compasses, and a scribe. The field of each panel was carved with a narrow-gauge chisel, at the discretion of the joiner, with considerable variety from maker to maker and time to time.

The lathe distinguished the turner from other workmen; turned furniture was made by rotating long pieces of roughly shaped wood between the two metal points of a lathe and cutting away the unwanted portion of the cylinder with a chisel known as a gouge or concave hollow. Turned cylinders were then assembled into furniture by fitting the rounded ends of crosspieces into auger holes drilled into upright members. The products—chairs,

Seventeenth-century oak chest in the Thomas Lee House, East Lyme, Connecticut. The oak box resting on its lid is English and dates from the same period.

footstools, spinning wheels, balusters, wooden plates called trenchers, pulleys for ships, and hubs for wheels—were generally known as turned work or "turnery." In the towns of England, the crafts of the joiner and the turner had been kept separate by the rules of the guilds, each of which jealously guarded the privilege of practicing its own "art and mysterie." But in New England furniture makers' guilds did not exist, so it was not unusual to find a turner and a joiner at work in the same shop—in some villages, the same craftsman was accomplished in both crafts.

At the end of the seventeenth century the cabinetmaker began to replace the joiner as the most important maker of furniture, first in England and later in America. The products of the cabinetmaker are easily distinguished from those of the joiner: the primary technique of the joiner is the pinned frame and panel, while the cabinetmaker uses board construction; where the primary joint of the joiner is the mortise and tenon, the cabinetmaker uses the dovetail; the primary ornamentations of the joiner are carving, planed grooves, applied spindles and moldings, and polychrome painting, while the cabinetmaker uses veneers; and where the joiner usually uses hardwood to frame his cases, the cabinetmaker commonly uses a conifer, like pine, under his veneer. The American strain of cabinetmaking, primarily using hardwoods rather than veneered softwoods, appeared after English-trained cabinetmakers introduced William and Mary–style furniture and construction techniques to New England.

Colonial American furniture still bears the marks of how it was made, and when. With the constant pressure to turn out as much work as possible, a colonial craftsman could not lavish workmanship on parts that would not be visible—the adage "time is money" had a grimly serious meaning. Tool marks were not removed from the bottoms and backs of drawers, the backs of case furniture, and inside joints. From the shape, texture, and quality of these marks, as well as from the woods and ornamentation used, one can often date and sometimes place colonial furniture.

By the time of settlement in America, the chest of drawers enjoyed great popularity. With storage space and a flat, fixed top on which articles such as glass and ceramics could be displayed, the chest of drawers was a functional and flexible object. An instance in which the contents of a seventeenth-century chest of drawers were itemized shows how broad its uses were. According to the New Hampshire Provincial Probate Records, in 1694 the "old Chest of drawers" of Ursulla Cutt of Portsmouth contained the following: its upper drawer held sewing equipment, glasses, jewelry, and some silver flatware; the second drawer held more jewelry, including gold rings and a pearl necklace, two small canvas tablecloths, and more textiles; the drawer below contained parcels of linens and other textiles; and the bottom drawer held sewing materials, clothing, sheets, and blankets, a looking glass, four earthenware dishes, and an old pewter pot.

New England Society Takes Shape:

Originally a Plantation of Religion, Not a Plantation of Trade

In 1630 John Winthrop wrote to his wife Margaret, who was still in England, "my deare wife, we are heer in a paradise." He was, of course, exaggerating. Yet even though America was not a paradise, it was a place where English men and women could free themselves from Stuart religious persecution and attempt to better their economic circumstances. With the reestablishment of the monarchy in England in 1660, a crucial issue for New England became population growth. The growth was the result not of continued migration from England (for that had largely ceased after 1640), but rather of natural increase. New England families were numerous, large, and long-lived. The region proved to be healthier than the mother country; while the birth rate was probably no higher than in England, the mortality rate for infants, children, and adults seems to have quickly fallen below that of England and Europe.

New England women could anticipate raising from five to seven healthy children, and their many children also produced many children, and subsequent generations followed suit. By 1700, New England's population had multiplied to approximately 100,000, and thirty years later that number had more than doubled. Such a dramatic phenomenon did not escape people's attention. As early as the 1720s, Americans pointed to their fertility, citing population growth as evidence of the advantages of living in the colonies, and in 1755 Benjamin Franklin published his *Observations, Concerning the Increase of Mankind*, which predicted that in another century "the greatest Number of Englishmen [would] be on this Side of the Water."

The expanding population clearly affected the two fundamental institutions of New England, the town and the church. For established towns, population growth meant intense pressure on town lands, and many members of the third and fourth generations were forced to migrate—north to New Hampshire or Maine, south to New York, west beyond the Connecticut River—to find farmland for themselves and their children. Others abandoned agriculture and learned skills like blacksmithing and carpentry, supporting themselves in the large number of new towns being founded.

This dispersal of population brought conflict between the newer and older settlements within the townships. Some men living at a distance from town objected to attending Sabbath services in the old meetinghouses or paying rates for highways and other services that they did not use. Records from this period reveal numerous disputes between men officially living in the same town but not feeling part of the same community. At the same time, the old system of open-field farming gave way to enclosed farms, and many inhabitants ceased to live on their house lots in the center of the original village. Population growth and dispersal splintered the old towns and weakened the social and political cohesion intended by the original Puritan founders.

Population growth also led, indirectly, to major changes in the church. Early Puritans had hoped that the world would be "remade out of the churches," and that the whole population of the Christian commonwealth would attain full membership in the church. But by the end of the seventeenth century, many young adults had failed to follow their parents and grandparents as full church members. This presented the gravest crisis that the colony had experienced. The situation seemed to be reverting to what the colonists had left behind in England: a minority of the truly godly surrounded by hordes of the unconverted. This, of course, threatened the cherished Puritan belief of the necessity for the churches to exercise discipline over their members.

For many clergy and godly laymen, the men who set the tone of public life and maintained that New England was essentially a "plantation of religion," the failure and degeneracy of the "rising generation" was a problem of social and religious order, discipline, and the survival of the churches. Leaders in New England reacted to the deterioration with laws and sermons that put God firmly on the side of the mercantile ideal. By this they attempted to make the individual serve both God and the community: Be not idle, for that is ungodly and antisocial. If you labor, labor for reasonable wages, for to take advantage of the shortage of labor is contrary to both God's word and society's good. Be not ostentatious wearing lace, for that is sinful and, because lace must be imported, detrimental to our economy. Do not sell goods for more than a "just price," for that is sinful and a crime against society. And do not hoard your wealth or squander it on frivolities, for God has given it to you to be used only for the good of the community. Laws and sermons could not stem the tide of secularization, however. Reverend Increase Mather, Cotton Mather's father, bemoaned this fact and reminded his congregation in 1676 that "it was with respect to some worldly accommodation, that other plantations were erected, but religion and not the world was that which our fathers came hither for." But Mather spoke for the past, not the future.

Puritan exhortations to work and economize did take deep root in New England, and the region saw a great growth of trade, wealth, and prosperity. By the 1670s, New England was deeply enmeshed in an intricate international trading network, ranging from the West Indies–centered rum-slave-sugar triangle to providing timber to the British Navy. And after the restoration of the Stuarts to the English throne, English merchants who were openly antagonistic to Puritan traditions began to migrate to New England. These new arrivals provided a style of life—liberal, secular, cosmopolitan—quite different from that of the Massachusetts Bay colony.

When we speak of New England, it should be clear that there was no single New England. Maine was still a frontier whose inhabitants hardily struggled to wrest a living from the soil, and New Hampshire was barely moving toward a society that could support a cultural life. Rhode Island could claim to have fostered certain distinctive political and religious ideas, but after 1660 little was added to the tenets of its founders and the colony lacked schools, colleges, and until 1727, a printing press. The Massachusetts Bay colony's ascendancy lay in its size and wealth, which allowed it to support Harvard College, the only institution of higher learning in New England until Yale College was founded in 1701. It also possessed the only printing press until 1709, when one was set up in New London. Boston was the center of New England bookselling and had the only concentration of men of learning, wealth, and some leisure in New England—a competitive, ostentatious "codfish aristocracy."

The New England economy, because of the limitations of a cold climate, rocky soil, low yields, and primitive transportation, was based on extractive industries related to the sea, forests, and commercial agriculture, supplying Atlantic islands and the West Indies with fish, corn, and wood. Each year the rising population

generated ever-greater demands for goods and services, which led to the development of small-scale colonial manufacturing and a complex network of internal trade. As the area of settlement expanded, new roads, bridges, mills, and stores were built to serve the new communities. And as the decades passed, it became more and more the goal of rural New Englanders to grow at least some products for the market in addition to their families' requirements. That they succeeded is evident in the lively coastal trade that developed: pork, cattle, horses, onions, boards, staves, pitch, and manufactured goods were sent to the West Indies and southern markets, ensuring economic health at home. By the late 1760s, more than half of the vessels leaving Boston Harbor were sailing to other colonies rather than to foreign ports; they were not only collecting goods for export and distributing imports but also selling items manufactured in New England.

Many New Englanders were ambivalent about this great economic success. The most visible symbol of this mixture of attitudes was the new pretentiousness of meetinghouse architecture—churches with soaring spires, richly carved interiors, high pulpits complete with paneled sounding boards, and brilliant cut-glass and brass chandeliers. The goal of these churches was unclear—on the one hand they celebrated God, on the other they showcased worldly prosperity. The men who stood in the pulpits and preached to the prospering merchants, tradesmen, and their families were themselves equivocal in their aspirations. They yearned to recapture the holiness of the early settlers and preached nostalgically of the golden age of the great migration. Scolding their congregations for the decline of virtue and faith, they exhorted them to reform and return to the simplicity and humility of their grandparents. A point of belief among many clergy was the danger of divine punishment if New Englanders did not remember, as Reverend John Higginson preached, "that New England is originally a plantation of Religion, not a plantation of Trade." While these sermons sincerely expressed feelings of fear, anxiety, and bewilderment during a time of change and controversy, they were preached as time-honored rituals by a clergy who themselves longed to cut figures of distinction in the world.

While voices prophesying doom cried out on many sides, a sense of a confident, incipient nationalism could be found in New England by 1700. The children and grandchildren of the first settlers now saw their America as a permanent and complete society, a distinct community identified with certain local institutions. As the eighteenth century progressed, the intense devotion to the Puritan past waned among ordinary farmers as well as among wealthier, more cosmopolitan people. In the port towns—Boston, Salem, Newbury, and a handful of others— commercial prosperity encouraged more and more involvement with the Atlantic trading world. Sailors speaking foreign languages and worshipping alien gods became part of the landscape in seaports. And while no such exotic influences were visible in country towns, secularism was rife among farmers, who marketed their surplus crops and gradually improved their living standard with imported luxuries.

This small late-seventeenth-century English spice chest is made of oak and deal wood. The sugar cone, nippers, and mortar and pestle, along with the spice chest, were used in everyday food preparation.

While laws and customs continued to give Congregationalism a privileged position within New England, they were gradually becoming more liberal and accommodating, allowing a variety of opinions. Anglicans, Baptists, and Quakers were gradually consolidating and expanding. As Congregationalism was shaped more by society, it acted less as a prime mover in that society. Although people were reluctant to admit it, Massachusetts had become pluralistic. The ideal of uniformity remained alive, but economic development had laid the foundation for a complex social order. While piety remained a powerful force, it had to compete with other values in a province that was economically integrated into a world of commerce. Church membership had so diminished that in most congregations only a minority of townspeople were members. Sexual morality, one indicator of piety in practice, had become so relaxed by the 1730s that in Massachusetts one-third to one-half of all first children being born were conceived out of wedlock. Community values were following individual behavior, not prescribing it.

Had they visited mid-eighteenth-century New England, Bradford and Winthrop would have mourned the distance that had widened between church and state, the diversity, the self-interested competition, and the great enthusiasm for worldly goods that gripped their progeny. Commerce, a pervasive day-to-day force, brought London tastes in architecture, furniture, fabrics, and ceramics to every village. Yankee culture and British culture— the one ascetic and oriented toward fulfilling the aspirations of the common farmers and tradesmen, the other elitist and cosmopolitan, aimed at refinement, excellence, and order—were rivals for the future domination of New England. British policy in the 1760s, culminating in the Stamp and Tea Acts, brought these two hitherto indistinct, parallel, and overlapping streams of social development into direct conflict, polarizing society as well as politics. Obedience to the British government came to signify an attachment to the hierarchical world of patronage and privilege; to preach resistance became emblematic of the Yankee heritage of Puritan ancestry, political autonomy, and the lean, thrifty ways of life practiced by independent freeholders. In the Revolution's concern for the common good, in the seriousness with which self-conscious republicans were eager to establish a republic of virtue, the world of Bradford and Winthrop's "Citty upon a Hill" endured.

Colonial Culture:

The Best of English Poetry and Prose

The great majority of eighteenth-century Americans— probably more than ninety percent—made their living as farmers. In 1720 the population of the five largest colonial cities—Boston, Newport, New York, Philadelphia, and Charleston—totaled about 36,000, only some seven percent of the entire population of the colonies. In 1760 the same cities numbered 73,000, a twofold growth, while the population as a whole had risen almost fourfold. In older, established regions, this population increase resulted in a mounting ratio of families to land, leading to the settlement of new communities in more distant areas. In the newly settled areas, agriculture provided almost the only activity, except for lumbering in northern New England. In such a society, divided between city and country, the culture was split: the older, traditional form was oral, communal, and intensely localized, while the newer culture of the commercial elite was print-oriented, more individualized, and self-consciously cosmopolitan.

A population that was substantially illiterate in the early seventeenth century was almost completely literate a hundred years later. The chief force behind this drive toward mass literacy was an intense and uniform Protestantism rather than changes in wealth or social position. In America pietism and rationalism flowed like two parallel currents in the same river, widely separated at the extremities but mingling in the center. The involvement of religion with utilitarian good works, education, and material progress is revealed in the stimulus given by the Great Awakening to the founding of schools and colleges. Following the earlier examples of Harvard (1636), William and Mary (1693), and Yale (1701), the colleges founded in the mid-eighteenth century—those now known as Princeton (1747), Columbia (1754), Brown (1765), and Rutgers (1766)—were originally intended to supply clergymen to fill the pulpits of Presbyterian, Anglican, Baptist, and Dutch Reformed churches, respectively. The founding of Dartmouth (1769), though not explicitly aimed at educating clerics, also had a religious purpose, that of Christianizing the Indians.

During the eighteenth century the curriculum and character of all these colleges changed considerably. Their students, the sons of the colonial elite, were now interested in careers in medicine, law, and business instead of the ministry. And the learned men who headed the colleges, though ministers themselves, were deeply affected by the Enlightenment. European intellectual currents had a dramatic effect on the colonial colleges, and they began to offer courses in mathematics, the natural sciences, law, and medicine.

The Enlightenment also had an enormous impact on well-to-do, educated Americans, supplying them with a common vocabulary and a unified view of the world, one that insisted that the rational eighteenth century was better than all previous ages. The immigration of well-trained and career-minded Presbyterians and Anglicans, as well as the return of Americans educated in Europe, brought home new ideas and a new professionalism. The teachings of the Scottish Enlightenment flowed into the colonies with the arrival of graduates of Glasgow University; other European-trained men provided a professional medical community and were responsible for founding hospitals and medical schools.

Accompanying the expansion of schools, colleges, libraries, clubs, and other learned manifestations of an expanding colonial culture were the voluminous products of the printing press. Many Americans gained their basic education from these, for they received little formal training. Among the most popular works published in the colonies was the annual almanac, containing astronomical and weather information, chronological tables, practical advice, and "the best of English poetry and prose." Various guides to every trade and vocation also sold well. Besides giving information on letter writing, commercial bookkeeping, and other useful skills, such books emphasized an optimistic, secular, and rational view of the world. Young men with ambition were advised to master skills that would enable them to adapt to and make their fortunes in a bustling, business-oriented world, advice that was almost always taken.

opposite page
The beamed-ceiling keeping room in Jefferds' Tavern in York, Maine, served as the eighteenth-century tavern's kitchen. It is furnished with everyday items that would be familiar to a colonial housewife, whose domain this would have been: coopered barrels and earthenware jars for the storage of foodstuffs and spices, sturdy work tables, simple chairs, and a ball-foot chest of about 1710 for the storage of linens and kitchen utensils.

Georgian Colonial Architecture in New England:

A Number of Fine Houses in the Great Road

In the years when the first contingents of settlers were arriving in the New World, another group of Englishmen left London for Italy to study Italian Renaissance architecture. Traveling with one group in 1613–14 was an artist of extraordinary talent, Inigo Jones. Jones took with him a copy of the North Italian sixteenth-century architect Andrea Palladio's *Four Books of Architecture,* in which he made marginal notes on the basic questions of proportion and detail. Returning to England, Jones promoted, with his refined taste and remarkable powers of synthesis, his own version of Renaissance architecture.

The isolated-block house developed in England was very different from its Italian prototype: there were no wings, no towers, no courtyards, and no interruptions of the horizontal line. A single door occupies the center of the long side, discreetly emphasized by a bracketed pediment; the windows are isolated against the clean wall and are symmetrical on either side of the door. The main block is terminated and contained by quoins at the corners and by a continuous cornice which, together with the string course between the floors, stresses the horizontal orientation of the building. Simplicity, wholeness, pristine clarity, and a pervasive symmetry are further emphasized by the hipped roof which pitches inward from all four sides and often terminates in a balustrade. Rhythmic variety is provided in the grouping of the principal windows, a theme carried into the roof by freestanding chimney stacks and dormers.

The double-pile house—two rooms deep, squarish in plan, of two or two-and-a-half stories and five (or, rarely, seven) sashed windows wide—appeared early in the eighteenth century in New England and persisted as the most common type for houses of any consequence down to the Revolution and beyond. It was a type that, having crystallized in England in the third quarter of the seventeenth century, was in a sense traditional by the time it crossed the Atlantic. Details and proportions throughout these houses are classical; in the subtlety with which independent units are related and joined, they convey something of the coherent unity of the classical temple.

After Inigo Jones died in 1652, the dominant figure in English architecture became Sir Christopher Wren. He brought to architecture a mind trained in mathematics and astronomy and demonstrated the capacity to think and work in large spatial terms, coherently and dramatically related. Moreover, because of his scientific background and practical ingenuity as a master mason, he had a command of materials and structure which went far beyond the capabilities of anyone else of his time, placing him among the greatest architect-engineers in the history of Western architecture. Wren's influence spread through virtually the entire fabric of English architecture, and this included colonial America, where his style was to assert itself in two building types in particular: the church and the detached house.

The Wren-baroque-style detached house in New England tended toward a stylistic unity between a rectangular block and a double- or single-pitch roof and gable ends. Although these houses vary in plan and detail, they share many common elements— symbols of material success essential to the New England merchant. They have a central door with a heavy segmental pediment on pilasters in one of the classical orders, made of wood rather than stone; the roof plane is broken by heavily scaled dormer windows with triangular and segmental pediments, a balustrade, and a cupola; and sometimes the rectangular mass has matched boards cut in imitation of rusticated masonry and sharply projecting quoined corners. A large central hall is paneled, sometimes from floor to ceiling, with regularly spaced pilasters and has an entablature with a heavy and richly carved modillion cornice. The principal rooms, which are arranged symmetrically around the central hall, are often similarly paneled. The decorative showpieces of the interior are the mantels, flanked by architectural pilasters and decorated with a deep frieze and sculptural panels carved with fruit and flower motifs. With the extravagant taste and pretentious elegance of the new architecture being built in New England coastal communities, they became thriving centers for woodworking craftsmen of every kind: carpenters, shipwrights, cabinetmakers, and carvers. The final chapter of the detached house of the Wren-baroque period was written in the New England backcountry and the upper Connecticut River valley where craftsmen, uninhibited by pattern-book knowledge, were free to exploit their own spirit of innovation and their own peculiar skills. In the hinterland, the bold and simple folk character of the houses, with their weathered clapboards and austere simplicity, gave them a strong seventeenth-century character well into the eighteenth century; but the symmetry of the facade, the classical details, and the large, elaborate baroque doors identify them with the eighteenth century.

After 1730, Georgian colonial architecture became more bookish due to the use of the builders' handbooks and architectural design books put out in considerable numbers by London publishers. This change in attitude, known as the Palladian movement, was a reaffirmation of classical principles as found in the work of Inigo Jones and Andrea Palladio. The Palladian movement was initiated by two significant books, Colen Campbell's *Vitruvius Britannicus* and an English translation of Palladio's *I quattro libri dell'architettura*, both published in 1714, at the very beginning of the Georgian era. Several other publications appeared which took up the theme and communicated Palladian ideas to the colonies; among the most important was James Gibbs's *A Book of Architecture*, first published in London in 1728, which appealed at once to the colonial taste. When William Salmon borrowed Palladio's name and published *Palladio Londinensis* in 1734, the feature that became most characteristic of the Palladian domestic style was the pedimented portico of one or two stories. These publications provided both architectural data, through engraved plates, and the theoretical basis of the Palladian movement.

Enthusiastic support for the style came from the Whig aristocracy, especially from Richard Boyle, Lord Burlington, whose patronage not only gave authoritative sanction to the new style, but whose own architectural works helped to shape its formal destiny. English Palladianism was a quest for absolutes and monumentality, and can thus be identified with the age of Enlightenment. Self-consciously severe and correct, the style is theoretically conceived in rigid geometric terms and was militantly antagonistic to the expansive richness and heaviness of the Wren-baroque. The various block units are symmetrically poised, one separate from the other, and are joined by straight connecting blocks similar to those found in the plates of Palladio's *Four Books*, where the wall planes are flat and tautly drawn against sharp corners, with doors and windows cleanly cut and isolated from one another. It was these qualities of exact dimensional definition, rigid balance, and staccato accentuation of the parts that were exploited by the

English Palladians. Classical details and proportion were all rendered strictly according to the Palladian doctrine.

These eighteenth-century design books show houses of the villa type with a dominating central component and symmetrical dependencies connected by straight or quadrant passages to form an open forecourt. James Gibbs was not a full-fledged Palladian; in his book he showed a preference for such rich baroque ornamental features as quoins, heavy rustication, pilasters, and balustrades; because of the popularity of his books in the colonies, it was these retardataire qualities that directed American architecture toward a form of Palladianism that never completely dissociated itself from the baroque richness of the Wren style of the first half of the century.

Doorway of the Old Parsonage, Newington, New Hampshire. In the New England backcountry and the offshoot coastal communities, the small, detached house of the Wren-baroque vernacular phase reached its ultimate dissemination in houses like this.

After mid-century the more ambitious houses in New England coastal cities began to reflect the Gibbsian version of English Palladian formalism. But there is not the slightest hint of the extended plan of alternating block units of the Palladian scheme; nowhere in New England is there a surviving example of a spread-out Palladian complex with central unit and attached dependencies, as there is in the South. Instead, the simple rectangular block with the monumental projecting pedimented pavilion and colossal pilasters enriched the facade and remained characteristic of the largest dwellings. Both inside and out, classical details were rendered with great authority; design books were the principal source for the new style. The continued predominance of wood, instead of brick and stone, not only imposed its own qualities on the classical forms but also impressed a definite regional stamp on New England houses. While traveling through northern Massachusetts in 1793, the observant antiquarian and Salem diarist Reverend William Bentley noted, "There are a number of fine houses in the great road which have a fine effect upon the Traveller, astonish him noticeably with the idea of ease by affluence. The Farms have great neatness, & convenience."

Nationalism, Cosmopolitanism, and Cultural Independence:

In Some Respects a Great Superiority

The first colonists had set out to construct a "little England"; what eventually resulted was a physical environment that bore only a resemblance to the English countryside and a society which, while appearing English, was in reality something quite different. By the middle of the eighteenth century, New England had a landed aristocracy that shared control of society with the merchant aristocracy of the cities. Social classes were sharply differentiated; the divisions were described just before the American Revolution by the author of *American Husbandry:* "The most ancient settled parts of the province of New England . . . contain many considerable land estates, upon which the owners live much in the style of country gentlemen in England . . . Here therefore we see a sketch of one class of people that has a minute resemblance to the gentle-

men of England who live upon their own estates, but they have in some respects a great superiority: they have more liberty in many instances, and are quite exempt from the overbearing influence of any neighboring noblemen."

The New England aristocracy was not burdened with the complicated ties of feudalism that remained in England. The stratification of society into the three classes of gentlemen, farmers, and the lower classes was accepted by everybody as a matter of course. What made it characteristically "American" was that it was so much easier to pass from one class to another, from a lower to a higher and vice versa. This made workers very industrious and beggars practically nonexistent. With industry and diligence almost any worker could look forward to the improved economic and social status that would come from ownership of land.

Large and small differences between England and the colonies are readily apparent in economics, the structure of land, labor, and in society, politics, religion, and the arts. One can also discern distinctions in language and education. The language of the Anglo-American reflected the polyglot nature of the colonial experience; it was an amalgam of English dialects with a sprinkling of Indian and African words and borrowings from a variety of European languages. There was also a greater interest in popular education than in England and Europe. In New England education was originally stressed for religious reasons, although in the eighteenth century the general virtue of an educated citizenry began to be recognized. The state acted; the notion of free public education took root, together with the embryonic thought that society owed everyone the ability to read and write.

In the middle and later years of the eighteenth century, Americans became more and more conscious of how different they were from Europeans. They stressed what they believed to be the uniqueness of their civilization with a boastfulness that naturally grated on the ears of traditional English groups. But the English were willing to grant to Americans, though reluctantly, a special mechanical aptitude. British periodicals told their readers about ingenious mechanics and the many machines being produced and perfected in America that revealed a mechanical proficiency that "far surpasses Europe." Lord Sheffield said that American axes were thought so superior that British manufacturers sold their own product as of New England make. Thomas Jefferson was protective of America's reputation in invention and the mechanical arts. New Jersey farmers, he said, had followed the practice of making the circumference of a wagon wheel of one single piece of wood. Benjamin Franklin suggested this procedure to a London workman and now, wrote Jefferson, it was claimed as an English invention. American hustle and bustle were fixed into the national grain; from Charleston, South Carolina, Dr. Alexander Garden wrote in 1764: "We are a set of the busiest, most bustling, hurrying animals imaginable."

As the seventeenth century wore into the eighteenth, merchants in the cities continued to amass wealth and develop tastes for the refinements of life, and the self-conscious interest in painting developed rapidly. As these provincial culture-seekers had turned to England for books, dress, furniture, and ideas, they also looked to the mother country for paintings and painters. Responding to this interest, a number of English painters saw fit to journey to America in the first half of the eighteenth century and were welcomed with open arms by the new American aristocracy. The most distinguished English artist to come to America in this period was John Smibert, who came to New England with Bishop Berkeley just at the moment when the American artistic mind was becoming conscious of itself and its interests.

In colonial America the native moods in art were strongly functional, but the more sophisticated mood was one of provincialism and cultural inferiority that resulted in a deliberate borrowing from Europe, and particularly England, of baroque art forms. However, against the studied baroque qualities of sensuousness, exaggeration, and over-ornamentation, seventeenth-century New England limners and their strict Calvinist patrons favored the mood of flat drawing and disciplined plainness inherited from Elizabethan England. American limners, who got their start painting houses, carriages, and tavern signs, began to paint likenesses of living people, excessively flat paintings of godly portrait subjects.

Americans' cultural self-consciousness was developing, and a deliberate effort at creativity and autonomy was unfolding. The Americans who understood and promoted a native tradition against imported English ways were the same people who favored an increasing measure of colonial autonomy in economics, politics, society, literature, and culture. Where English achievement was too exclusively aristocratic, as in painting, no strong development could be expected in early colonial society, unburdened by a hereditary aristocracy. But where English traditions in the arts and crafts were of a high order, as in silversmithing and cabinetmaking, colonial standards revealed not only the imprint of the parent pattern but also the growth toward mature self-direction.

The ascendancy of American autonomy in the decorative arts was visible throughout New England. Long recognized as one of the major eighteenth-century centers of furniture making in America, Boston had hundreds of workmen plying their trades in small shops throughout the town. In 1750 James Birket, an English traveler from the West Indies, found Boston filled with craftsmen; to him, their number surpassed that in any other American town: "The Artificers in this Place Exceed Any upon ye Continent And are here also Most Numerous as Cabinet Makers, Chace & Coach Makers . . . Watchmakers, Printers, Smith, & C." When Andrew Burnaby, Vicar of Greenwich, England, traveled through New England in 1760, he was impressed by the gentle elegance and artistic temper of the inhabitants: "The arts are undeniably forwarder in Massachusetts Bay, than either in Pennsylvania or New York. The public buildings are more elegant; and there is a more general turn for music, painting, and the belles lettres." The patrons of these arts were wealthy merchants whose impressive fortunes were often reflected in a fine domestic display. The home of such a merchant, obviously a composite of native craftsmanship and imported wares, was described by John Adams in 1766: "Dined at Mr. Nick Boylstones . . . Went over the House to view the Furniture, which alone cost a thousand Pounds sterling. A Seat it is for a noble Man, a Prince. The Turkey Carpets, the painted Hangings, the Marble Tables, the rich Beds with crimson Damask Curtains and Counterpins, the beautiful Chimny Clock, the Spacious Garden, are the most magnificent of any Thing I have ever seen."

Boylston and his peers surrounded themselves with the latest fashions, and the ruling style in Boston from about 1730 until 1765 was the style known today as Queen Anne—a style with a basic reliance on sweeping curves and symmetrical movement. During the fifty-year period prior to the Revolution, the two furniture forms that were particularly distinctive and popular in Massachusetts were block-front and bombé casepieces. The former was defined by the alternate raising and depressing of vertical facade panels; the latter by a single bulge located near the base of the front and sides of the piece. Another unique characteristic of Boston furniture during this period was a form of surface decoration known as japanning, or Indian work—a simplified imitation of Oriental lacquerwork. New England urban furniture is characterized by richness, rationality, classic proportions, and an uncompromising symmetry. Not only did skilled furniture makers supply furniture and furnishings to local homes, they also maintained an extensive export trade, sending both plain and fancy wares to coastal ports and to the West Indies. That craftsmen took advantage of the mercantile activity of intercoastal trade is documented by a newspaper advertisement by Plunkett Fleeson, a Philadelphia upholsterer, who advertised in 1742 that his chairs were "cheaper than any made here, or imported from Boston."

During the 1750s and 1760s there were growing signs of an awakening cultural self-consciousness and deliberate efforts by craftsmen, artists, and littérateurs to make a place for Americans in the cultural sun. It is from this period that there is much evidence of a growing American self-assertiveness and national feeling, a growing sense of the potential grandeur and power of the America of the future. Benjamin Franklin was beginning to see in America the very heart and center of the culture of Western civilization; he wrote to Mary Stevenson in 1763: "After the first Cares for the Necessaries of Life are over, we shall come to think of the Embellishments. Already some of our young Geniuses begin to lisp Attempts at Painting, Poetry and Musick." And it was in this period that expansionists like John Adams began to sing America's manifest destiny to dominate the continent. In 1765 the young Adams saw America as somehow chosen by God as the instrument of bringing happiness to humankind. He wrote: "I always consider the settlement of America with reverence and wonder, as the opening of a grand scene and design in Providence for the illumination of the ignorant and the emancipation of the slavish part of mankind all over the earth."

This American nationalism was not at first a nationalism of independence; it was a nationalism that expected to find self-expression within the framework of the Empire. But given Americans' convictions and mood, given, that is, a self-respect and pride that made submission to George III and his ministers

impossible, the Revolution could hardly have been avoided—the thirteen British colonies had become a nation. Patrick Henry, like so many other Americans fired by the discovery of his own America and driven to desperation by the inability of Britain to comprehend the nationhood of America, burst out his famous cry: "The distinction between Virginians, Pennsylvanians, New Yorkers, and New Englanders are no more. I am not a Virginian, but an American."

Simple pews in the German Lutheran Church in Waldoboro, Maine.

The interior of the German Lutheran Church in Waldoboro is strikingly compartmentalized. The proprietors of the new Maine townships varied considerably in motives, wealth, and the manner in which they acquired their holdings, but the sudden expansion of the Maine frontier can generally be attributed to land speculation.

Maine's settlement ran close to the coast, sprinkled along the rivers of the region; in 1760 the population numbered only about 20,000. But the enormous resources in the state's forests and rivers and increasingly crowded conditions in southern New England would soon draw thousands more to the frontier.

View of the Parson Capen House in Topsfield, Massachusetts. The house frame in the seventeenth century could be simple and box - like, or its mass could be more complex, the profile of the individual surfaces broken with oversailing upper stories. Common in the second half of the century was the carved pendant drop that ornaments this overhang. These bursts of decorative exuberance were confined almost entirely to the last quarter of the seventeenth century, within the context of New England's first architectural coming-of-age. With the frame of the house raised and the chimney stack constructed, it was essential in the New England climate that the structure be covered with clapboarded walls and shingled roofs. Most New England houses were also glazed from the outset. In 1629, Francis Higginson reminded his friends in England to be sure to "furnish yourselves with . . . glass for windows," and William Wood advised prospective planters in 1634 that "Glasse ought not to be forgotten of any that desire to benefit themselves, or the Countrey."

The Parson Capen House, 1683, is typical of the first houses erected by the New England colonists. These structures naturally reflected the Elizabethan half-timbered homes the colonists left behind in southeastern England, and include such typical seventeenth-century features as precipitously sloping roofs, rectangular (rather than square) chimney tops, casement windows with leaded panes, and overhanging second stories.

Early New England houses, such as the Whipple House, Ipswich, Massachusetts, built about 1640, had frames of heavy hand-hewn timbers, usually oak, held together by mortise-and-tenon joints secured by wooden pegs. In Essex County, Massachusetts, oak had become so scarce by 1660 that the town of Ipswich was forced to issue felling grants to those who wanted to cut a white oak tree, with a ten-shilling penalty for every tree cut without permission. In their structural characteristics, these early New England houses showed no variation from traditional English practices. The oak frame was stiffened by angle braces at the corners and by heavy beams called chimney girts which ran completely across the house, abutting the chimney on either side. From these chimney girts to the main girts on either side of the house ran another huge structural member, the summer beam. ("Summer" was derived from "sumpter," a pack horse which was capable of bearing great weight.) The summer beam here has a chamfer, or beveled edge.

View of the Whipple House, built about 1639. The first Massachusetts settlers were English, and these men and women never wholly ceased to be English. The seventeenth-century vernacular houses in Massachusetts clearly enunciate the close relationship between the buildings the immigrants had grown up in and those they erected upon their arrival in the New World. There were normally two entrances, front and back; as yet untainted by classicism, these doors were located well off center.

preceding pages

The kitchen of the John Alden House, built by John Alden and his son, Jonathan, in 1653, is believed to be part of the Duxbury house Alden built soon after he received his land grant in 1627. John and Priscilla Mullins Alden lived in Duxbury for about twenty-five years before moving into this house, where they remained until their deaths. In 1632 the colonists in Duxbury asked to be dismissed from the Plymouth church and to be allowed to establish their own; Elder William Brewster, who had led the Separatists from England to Holland in 1608 and to the New World in 1620, gathered the new church, the first to break away from the Plymouth congregation. Governor William Bradford did dismiss the Duxbury settlers from Plymouth, "though very unwillingly."

The Paul Revere House, North Square, Boston, Massachusetts, built 1676–81 and altered at various times thereafter, was bought in 1681 by Robert Howard, a leading Boston merchant. Between Howard's death in 1718 and 1770, the property passed through the hands of several owners, and in 1770 it was sold to Paul Revere. In the early 1740s the ell on the house, whose previous purpose is unknown, was converted into a kitchen by the addition of a chimney and fireplace, both of which still survive. The pent roof was added about 1850 when a tenement (since demolished) was built immediately adjacent to the house.

opposite page

The kitchen of the Paul Revere House, on the ground floor of the ell, displays some standard utensils for food preparation. On January 27, 1775, the secretary of state for America, Lord Dartmouth, addressed a letter to General Gage in Boston, which reached him on April 14th. Expressing his belief that American resistance was nothing more than the response of a "rude rabble without a plan," Dartmouth ordered Gage to arrest "the principal actors in the provincial congress." Gage sent an expedition to confiscate provincial military supplies stockpiled at Concord; Bostonians dispatched two messengers, William Dawes and Paul Revere, to rouse the countryside. When the British vanguard approached Lexington at dawn on April 19th, they found a group of militiamen drawn up on the town common—the American Revolution was born.

The Paul Revere House is the only survivor of many such row houses found in late-seventeenth-century Boston. The Revere House is a building of great architectural sophistication: it had painted graining and lath and plaster ceilings, which survive on the second floor. The hall, which comprises the entire ground floor of the main house, is furnished to the period of Paul Howard's occupancy.

The maple gateleg table and oak side and arm chairs were made in Massachusetts, 1680–1700; the walnut high chest of drawers was made in Boston, 1700–1720, and has elegant inlay around the drawers. The mixture of styles and of English and American pieces of furniture is characteristic of Boston interiors throughout the colonial period.

The kneehole desk from the Paul Revere Memorial Association, North Square, Boston, Massachusetts, is a fine example of early Boston furniture-making. It was made about 1720 of burl walnut veneer on walnut.

opposite page

This view of the staircase in the Pierce-Hichborn House, North Square, Boston, Massachusetts, built about 1711, shows such characteristic features of late-seventeenth- and early-eighteenth-century English architecture as the acorn drops at the bottom of the upper newels and the juxtaposition of a balustrade and inclined sides of the stair. The heavy dado ends at the second-floor landing, but the balustrade is carried past the third floor into the attic crawl-space. If the Paul Revere House looks back to the timber-frame houses of Elizabethan England, its neighbor across the courtyard, the brick Pierce-Hichborn House, looks forward to the English Georgian style. The Revere House was preserved because of its historic associations; the Pierce-Hichborn House, a superior example of early-eighteenth-century middle-class taste, was preserved largely by chance.

This second-floor room in the Pierce-Hichborn House is furnished as a parlor. Built for Moses Pierce about 1711, the house was bought in 1781 by Nathaniel Hichborn, a cousin of Paul Revere, and it remained in the family for more than eighty years. Moses Pierce was a glazier, and the immense double-hung sash windows, which were just then becoming fashionable, testify to the state of the glazier's art in Boston at the time. This room has been furnished as a parlor from Nathaniel Hichborn's 1795 inventory; by this time colonial eclecticism in furnishings had intensified due to an expanding trade in new and old furniture. In Hichborn's inventory the room contained the only chest in the house, represented here by the New England maple high chest of drawers of about 1720; the daybed is possibly American and made about 1700. The wallpaper is a modern reproduction made from fragments found during the restoration of the house.

The austere furnishings in this second-floor bedroom in the Pierce-Hichborn House reflect conditions and tastes during the Federal period, when, according to Hichborn's inventory, this room had the only bedstead in the house. The heavy bolection molding around the fireplace is original, as is the mantel shelf, and is characteristic of early-eighteenth-century detailing.

preceding page

In 1635 a group of "God-fearing Puritans," seeking the freedom to worship and govern themselves, sailed into a sheltered bay twelve miles southeast of Boston, led by the Reverend Peter Hobart of Hingham, Norfolk, England. They landed near the present harbor and formed the core of the new plantation; in 1635 the Great and General Court in Boston recognized the settlement, named it Hingham, and incorporated it as the twelfth town in the Massachusetts Bay Colony. In 1681 the First Parish Meetinghouse, later known as the Old Ship Meetinghouse, was built. In 1727 residents of South Hingham, vexed by having to travel so far to attend services at the Old Ship Meetinghouse, petitioned the Great and General Court for their own parish. Still without permission in 1742, they erected this meetinghouse, the Second Parish Church of Hingham, Massachusetts. In keeping with the Puritan practice, the entrance was on the long side and the pulpit opposite; the entrance was moved to the front of the church in 1829.

While serving the last year of a tutorship at Yale in 1734, the Reverend John Sergeant accepted an offer from the Boston Commission on Indian Affairs, an agency of the London Society for the Propagation of the Gospel in New England, to establish a mission among the Housatonic Indians in southern Berkshire County. Several colonists and their families moved to Stockbridge in 1737, built a stockade, and set about to serve as models of the English way of life. A narrow passage containing the chimney lies behind the pine paneling in the west bedroom of the Mission House, Stockbridge, Massachusetts, presumably for insulation against the north wind. The chest of quartered oak with ebonized bosses and spindles was probably made in eastern Massachusetts about 1640.

The kitchen in the Mission House, Stockbridge, Massachusetts, begun in 1739 and completed some years later, contains the largest of the four fireplaces in the house. On display are American culinary and domestic utensils of the eighteenth and nineteenth centuries and, above the mantel, a French musket of the mid-eighteenth century.

opposite page
The transitional side chairs with Spanish feet and the sawbuck table set with treen in the kitchen of the Mission House are from the Carver family of Plymouth, Massachusetts. The pine cupboard, probably made in New York State about 1740–80, contains eighteenth- and nineteenth-century British and American pewter, tin, and earthenware.

The Reverend John Sergeant's study in the Mission House, Stockbridge, Massachusetts, is hung with mezzotints of eighteenth-century clergymen. Included among them is the Reverend Benjamin Coleman, who, with Jonathan Belcher, governor of Massachusetts and New Hampshire, advanced Sergeant the money to build the Mission House. The New England armchair belonged to Sergeant and was bought from a direct descendant. The salt-glazed-stoneware-and-pewter inkwell, dated 1701, sits on a maple-and-pine table from about 1700–1720.

The children's room in the Mission House is the only room in the house without a fireplace. The mottled appearance of the walls was created by a wash of buttermilk, eggs, and soot. The township of Stockbridge was incorporated in 1739, the same year John Sergeant married Abigail, the eldest daughter of Ephraim Williams. A forthright eighteen-year-old unused to the rigors of the wilderness, she made clear her intent to have a fine house.

46

Rocky Hill Meetinghouse, Amesbury, Massachusetts, was built in 1785 to serve the west parish of Salisbury (now Amesbury). New England communities were remarkable for their extraordinarily homogeneity. The center of each town was the green or common, and in a prominent position on the green stood the meetinghouse, a unique architectural type which served not only the religious life of the community but its social and civic needs as well.

Here the entire town came together and expressed itself in all its affairs. But the meetinghouse was first of all a house of worship, and had its origin in the religious practices of the New England Puritans. In exalting sobriety and purity, they developed a wholly new concept of church edifice.

opposite page

The Manse in Monterey, Massachusetts, is near Great Barrington in the steeply sloping upland hills of Berkshire County, west of the broad floodplain of the central Connecticut River valley. The thin, rocky soil of the upland farms is now thickly forested with hardwoods and a substantial complement of conifers. The first settlers came to the Berkshires after the end of Queen Anne's War in 1713. They avoided the damp valleys shaded by stands of white pine and built their towns and farmsteads on well-drained hillsides, which offered the best pasturage. By the 1750s trade prospered, agriculture flourished, and noble clapboard houses, like the Manse, were built. They survive today as durable monuments to an earlier era of agricultural prosperity.

The General Sylvanus Thayer Birthplace in Braintree, Massachusetts, was built in 1720 by Thayer's great-grandfather and enlarged in 1755. Sylvanus Thayer was born here in 1785, graduated from Dartmouth College in 1807, and in 1817 was made superintendent of West Point. He became known as the "Father of the Military Academy" for turning it into a well-run, disciplined institution with high scholastic standards. He also built military fortifications along the eastern seaboard, designed and donated the Thayer School of Engineering at Dartmouth, and was the benefactor of Thayer Academy and the Thayer Public Library in Braintree. Upon his retirement from the army he returned to Braintree, where he died in 1863.

The wallpaper of the parlor of the General Sylvanus Thayer Birthplace in Braintree, Massachusetts, is a reproduction of the original pre-Revolutionary paper, and the furniture in the room is of New England origin. To the left of the late-eighteenth-century upholstered easy chair is a rare maple tripod, a snake-foot candle-stand with a wind shield, and to the right, a maple tilt-top table. The maple banister-back chair of 1700–1720 belonged to Sylvanus Thayer's mother, Dorcas Faxon (1756–1840). The pine corner cupboard, filled with pewter, was made about 1760–70 and was found in Maine. In the foreground is a pine and maple porringer-top table, stained black, set with a Britannia teapot, a pewter hot-water urn, painted black, and a set of English transfer-printed creamware tea bowls and saucers of about 1765.

opposite page
The New England maple bed of 1790–1800 in a bedroom of the General Sylvanus Thayer Birthplace is stained red; on it are a copperplate-printed quilt and a calamanco quilt. The bed hangings are modern reproductions. Below the New England mahogany Chippendale looking glass is a pine blanket chest painted dark green. Also of New England origin are the pine chest at the foot of the bed and the mahogany cradle. Between the windows a courting mirror hangs over a small slant-front pine desk, probably made in eastern Connecticut about 1750. Flanking the desk and the simple maple corner chair are a maple side chair and a red-stained bow-back Windsor chair, all New England.

50

This room, known as the hall, of the General Sylvanus Thayer Birthplace, was originally used for many purposes, including cooking. In the corner of the room is a late-seventeenth-century folding bed complete with bed key and fid (a hardwood pin used in opening the strands of a rope), hand-woven sheets and blankets, a corn-husk mattress, and a feather bed; the crewel hangings were worked recently. Next to the bed is a Flemish oak armchair with a caned seat and back of around 1700. In front of the window is a New England oak turned tavern table, about 1750, on which are a rush light, a tinderbox, books, and an English pewter inkstand.

In the foreground is a New England chair-table set with English and American pewter, surrounded by four Cromwellian chairs with leather seats and backs and turned front legs that were probably made in Boston or the Connecticut River valley about 1650–60.

opposite page
Original red-painted sheathing surrounds a huge five-by-seven-foot fireplace, with a beehive brick oven in the back, in the large kitchen in the lean-to that was added in 1755 to the General Sylvanus Thayer Birthplace.

The press cupboard in the General Sylvanus Thayer Birthplace is attributed to the shop of John Emery (d. 1683) of Newbury, Massachusetts. Made of oak and tulip poplar, it is incised in the lower drawer "E.P." On top of the casepiece are a pair of English pewter candlesticks, an oval English pewter platter, and a Continental pewter tureen, all made in the eighteenth century.

Children's toys and furniture in the second floor of the lean-to.

opposite page
The modifications made in the 1750s to the Dwight-Barnard House, built in Springfield, Massachusetts, 1722–33, included the gambrel roof, pedimented dormers, distinctive Connecticut River valley doorway and window surrounds, and the polychrome paint scheme. The house was reerected in Deerfield in 1954. More expensive colonial dwellings were often adorned with pediments; sources for such doorways and window cornices can be found in architecture pattern books. In October 1830 the *Greenfield Gazette* described Deerfield as consisting of "about 70 or 80 houses, mostly white," but at mid-century Andrew Jackson Downing disparaged the increasingly popular green-and-white color scheme as "frequently employed by house painters."

56

opposite page

The parsonage of the First Church of Deerfield, Massachusetts, was built by Jonathan Hoyt in 1775 in Cheapside (an industrial portion of Deerfield annexed by neighboring Greenfield in 1896), and reerected in Deerfield in 1965. In the winter of 1782, the Reverend William Bentley of Salem observed in his diary that there were in Deerfield "about 60 houses in the Street in better style than in any of the Towns I saw." Deerfield today is a picturesque village on a little plateau in the Connecticut River valley, its buildings mostly set along "the street," which is broad and shaded by old elms. The Federal style emerged in Deerfield first in alterations and additions to old houses, as in the doorway to the Parsonage; later houses in the region were much influenced by the design books of Asher Benjamin, the *Country Builder's Assistant* (1797) and *American Builder's Companion* (1806).

John Quincy Adams was born in this room on July 11, 1767, now the John Quincy Adams Birthplace in Quincy, Massachusetts. His father, John Adams, a lawyer as well as a farmer, was drawn increasingly into public life as the Revolution approached. Before, during, and after the war he was away from home a great deal; his wife, Abigail, kept him abreast of the situation in embattled Boston. The letters she wrote to him during those years emphasize the simplicity of the Adamses' life in the little houses in Braintree (now Quincy); greatness did not separate them from their world. After she joined her husband in Europe in the late 1780s, she wrote home: "I long to return to my native land. My little cottage encompassed with my friends has more charms for me than the drawing rooms of St. James."

View of the kitchen in the lean-to of the John Quincy Adams Birthplace, built in 1663 and enlarged in 1716. The history of the Adams family in America begins in 1638, when yeoman Henry Adams came to Massachusetts from England. In 1720 Henry's great-grandson, Deacon John Adams, purchased this property on the Boston and Plymouth Highway. There, in a larger house, he lived with his wife, Susannah Boylston, and had a son, John, who was to become the second president of the United States. In 1764 John Adams married Abigail Smith of the neighboring town of Weymouth and brought his bride to the smaller house on the property—this house—and there they made their home for most of the next twenty-four years. In 1767 John Quincy Adams, later the sixth president of the United States, was born here.

The Old Manse in Concord, Massachusetts, built as a parsonage by the Reverend William Emerson in 1769–70, still looks very much as it did when it was new, except for the gabled window built into the roof by the Reverend Samuel Ripley in 1845. "Among the houses of Concord," wrote Franklin B. Sanborn, a friend and biographer of many of New England's greatest writers, "Old Manse has had the most romantic history." Nathaniel Hawthorne made this charming house forever famous in his *Mosses from an Old Manse*.

following page

On a sunny morning the bull's-eye glass panes above the front door of the Old Manse make a swirling pattern of the brilliant autumn foliage. Ralph Waldo Emerson lived in the Old Manse in the mid-1830s. Describing the pickerelweed blooming in the shallow margins of the river and the swarms of butterflies in continual motion outside the window of his study, he wrote, "Art cannot rival this pomp of purple and gold."

The tiger-maple chest of drawers in the dining room of the Manse in Monterey, Massachusetts, was made in that state about 1720–30, and was originally the top section of a high chest of drawers. Arranged on its top are wrought-iron and paktong candelabra and a silver-plated cruet stand and salt cellars. The eighteenth century saw a steady improvement in the quality of housing in city and country, reflecting the rising standard of living in a prosperous, fluid society. Wood was still the principal element of construction, though brick was increasingly used in the houses of the gentry. By the 1750s the coastal seaports favored a colonial Georgian style based on British architectural styles, which were in turn based on the columns, friezes, pediments, and other decorative devices of ancient Greece and Rome. Only on the frontier did housing still reflect earlier methods and styles.

following pages

View of the west bedroom of the Manse. After the Revolution the interests of the prosperous urban merchants and market farmers in the eastern counties of Massachusetts were different from those of the semi-subsistence farmers and sheep farmers in the poorer upland towns of western Massachusetts. Issues such as taxation, inflation, and the administration of justice were the subject of clamorous debate, leading to a rebellion in Hampshire County in 1786. In neighboring Berkshire County in 1784, a mob estimated at 2,000 prevented the Court of Common Pleas from sitting in Great Barrington. The insurrections demonstrated the necessity for a truly national government, one able to coin money, levy taxes, and keep the peace. So when the Philadelphia Convention drafted a new United States Constitution and offered it to the states for adoption, it was a Berkshire countryman, Jonathan Smith, who persuaded the farmers in the Massachusetts legislature to adopt it.

View of the east bedroom of the Manse, built in 1750 for Adonijah Bidwell, the first minister in Monterey and a graduate of Yale College. Bidwell was a prosperous man; the estate inventory taken upon his death lists five looking glasses, eight beds, many chairs, including eighteen heart-and-crown chairs and three roundabout chairs, lots of pewter, including fifty plates, and a large library. The New England armchair in the foreground dates from the eighteenth century. The bed hangings are modern Indian crewelwork, but the American linsey-woolsey coverlet dates from the late eighteenth century.

The Boston and Sandwich Glass Company, Sandwich, Massachusetts, made the pressed glass in the King Caesar House, Duxbury, Massachusetts, built for Ezra Weston Jr. in 1808 and 1809. All the glassware is in the cable pattern made to commemorate the landing at Duxbury in 1869 of the French Atlantic Cable, the first direct telegraph cable from continental Europe to the United States.

65

This mid-seventeenth-century room in the Gilman Garrison House, Exeter, New Hampshire, was constructed with a plain heavy summer beam, scratch-molded joists, and a puncheon floor (split logs with the faces smoothed). The oak side table is English. In October 1641 the Massachusetts General Court ordered, "with the Consent of the inhabitants of the said ryver," that all the persons settled at "the ryver of the Pascataquack" were "accepted and reputed under the government of Massachusetts, as the rest of the inhabitants within the said jurisdiction are." After 1641 and until September 1643, Exeter remained the only New Hampshire town outside the Bible Commonwealth.

This bedchamber in the Gilman Garrison House, Exeter, New Hampshire, is part of a mid-eighteenth-century addition. The crewel embroidered bed hangings are reproduced from fragments of a set used in Exeter; the four-post bed is also a reproduction. The Chippendale commode chair is probably English. The oval Federal looking glass belonged to Elizabeth Clifford, who lived in the house, and is probably the "gilt-fram'd looking glass" mentioned in a later inventory. Peter Gilman died in 1788, and to settle the estate the house was sold to Ebenezer Clifford. An ingenious entrepreneur, Clifford set up a small factory in the house for making tall-case clocks and various other inventions and also took in as boarders a few students from the newly established Phillips Exeter Academy. One boy who arrived to board here in 1798 was Daniel Webster, later a great American statesman.

The German Lutheran Church in Waldoboro, Maine, was built in 1773 and moved and reerected in 1795. The building is a variant of the New England meetinghouse type, with the exception that the pulpit is at the end of a long axis opposite an entry housing the gallery stairs. Unlike the standard arrangement, the entrance is at the gable end of the building, as in a traditional church.

In 1730 the Lincolnshire Company, led by Samuel Waldo, a Boston merchant, land speculator, and politician, received a grant of land between the Penobscot and Muscongus rivers from the Council for New England. Waldo called the resulting township Waldoboro, and brought a number of German Protestant families to settle, till the land, and manufacture iron and lime here.

Some of the headstones in the Old Burying Ground next to
Jefferds' Tavern in York, Maine, date from the seventeenth century;
here also is a mass grave with the remains of forty York residents
killed in the predawn Indian Massacre of Candlemas Day in 1692.

opposite page

When the Emersons enlarged the Emerson-Wilcox House in York, Maine, in the decade prior to the American Revolution, access between the two sections that were joined was created by cutting through the center chimney of the original structure, creating this vaulted passageway directly opposite the front entry. The closeness of the winding rough plaster walls and the varying arches of the ceiling evoke the vernacular quality of Elizabethan architecture.

The John Hancock Wharf and Warehouse in York, Maine, was built along the York River in the 1760s. From York's first settlement in 1624 through the latter part of the nineteenth century, shipping played an important role in the town's development. For nearly 250 years, vessels sailed in and out of York Harbor and the Cape Neddick River, supplying the area with goods from all over the world. Between 1763 and the Revolutionary War, York had several prosperous merchants, such as Jonathan Sayward and Edward Emerson, trading with the West Indies. In 1789 the federal government named York a port of delivery for the first district of Maine, and the John Hancock Warehouse served for an extended period as the customshouse for the port.

The Old Gaol in York, Maine, was built in 1720 as the King's
Prison in the Province of Maine. Legislation for the establishment
of a royal prison was enacted in 1653, and after some delay a
building for this purpose was erected in 1656 at Meetinghouse
Creek in York. The present Gaol was built in 1720 from timbers
salvaged from the original structure. With the great mid-eighteenth-
century influx of settlers, the building was enlarged in 1760, 1799,
and 1806 to provide more space for the housing of prisoners, as
well as to improve accommodations for the jailer's family. It served
as a jail until 1860.

The humanitarian drive for better prison conditions for debtors following the Revolution resulted in the addition of this large debtor's cell to the Old Gaol in York, Maine, in the 1790s, giving the building its present shape. Spartan and foreboding, the cell is furnished with a cobbler's bench; those put into prison for debt were expected to work while incarcerated, both to pay off their outstanding debts and to cover their boarding charge while in jail.

After 1860 the Gaol served briefly as a school, boarding house, and warehouse; by 1895 it stood abandoned and neglected until William Dean Howells, a summer resident of York Harbor and editor of the *Atlantic Monthly*, started a preservation movement to restore the Old Gaol and convert it into a "museum of colonial relics." On hand for the opening celebration on July 1, 1900, were such luminaries as Thomas Nelson Page and Mark Twain.

The Emerson-Wilcox House in York, Maine.

Since 1954 the Emerson-Wilcox House has been a part of the Old Gaol Museum, presenting local history and reflecting changing tastes in domestic interiors in York since the 1740s. This small parlor illustrates a typical southern Maine interior from the period prior to the Revolution, with a 1750 portrait of an unidentified woman by John Greenwood hanging above a Queen Anne–period circular drop-leaf table made by Samuel Sewall, a local cabinet-maker. The Chippendale side chair, one of six in the room and part of a large set of eighteen, was made in Portsmouth after 1763 for Nathaniel Barrell, a local merchant.

74

The earlier section of the Emerson-Wilcox House adjoins the original kitchen and functioned for a time as a tavern room. It retains its early shutters and corner fireplace with fielded-panel breastwork. During the 1930s, descendants of the original owners used the dwelling as a summer home and rearranged the room as an elegant colonial-revival dining room, using family heirlooms from the Federal period. Shown here set for afternoon tea, the room bespeaks pride in a consciously preserved and revered colonial past.

opposite page

Hamilton House, in South Berwick, Maine, sits prominently on a bluff overlooking the tidal Piscataqua River and its tributaries. The classically proportioned house eloquently illustrates Colonel Jonathan Hamilton's stature as the most prominent merchant in the region as well as the community's economic orientation to maritime commerce. The roof was originally capped with a balustrade, and the house was surrounded by farmland, sheds, a barn, spinning house, and slave quarters.

The front, or southwest, parlor of Hamilton House, South Berwick, Maine, has a pair of broad arches with elaborately carved keystones. According to the estate inventory taken after Colonel Jonathan Hamilton's sudden death in 1802, this room was furnished with a sofa, twelve chairs, two easy chairs, tea and card tables, a pair of large looking glasses, a Brussels carpet, and one picture—what one status-conscious gentleman considered necessary for his comfort.

After Emily Tyson toured Italy in 1905, she ordered murals of Italian gardens and classical ruins painted in the dining room of Hamilton House. But Mrs. Tyson's greatest contribution to the property was the creation of a formal garden; an avid gardener, she favored traditional plantings laid out in symmetrical beds.

Trellises, arbors, sundials, and statuary were interspersed among the stately flower beds. The plan was designed to extend the house into the garden so that leisurely summer activities could move easily between indoors and out; the murals, painted by George Porter Fernald, unite the dining room with the garden just outside.

opposite page

The wallpaper of the stair hall of Hamilton House is a late-nineteenth-century English or American reproduction of Colonel Hamilton's original pillar-and-arch wallpaper, probably made in Boston about 1787. Round-headed windows with deep window seats were favored throughout the Piscataqua region. The tall-case clock on the stair landing was made by Benjamin Cox of Philadelphia, 1809–13.

The parlor chamber of Hamilton House was decorated in the colonial-revival style by Emily Tyson, the widow of the president of the Baltimore and Ohio Railroad. Tyson bought Hamilton House at the end of the nineteenth century and, with the restoration help of the Boston architect Herbert Browne, gave the house a grand and picturesque interpretation of the colonial era. Typical of colonial revival proponents, she collected Federal furniture, country and fancy painted furniture, straw matting and hooked rugs, Sandwich colored glass, ship models, and Currier and Ives prints—all evocative of a romanticized past.

The dining room of Hamilton House boasts a splendid view over a tributary of the Piscataqua River. The banjo clock hanging on the wall was made in Boston or Salem about 1825.

The Hamilton House, situated on a bluff overlooking a tributary of the Piscataqua River, affords an expansive view from this second-floor window. The river and its tributaries served as highways for the local gentry, who traveled in their own pleasure barges called river coaches. When Colonel Jonathan Hamilton built his house around 1787, it overlooked prosperous warehouses and bustling shipyards. Hamilton had risen from humble beginnings to become the most prominent merchant in the region, exporting timber from inland New Hampshire and Maine and importing rum, molasses, and slaves from the West Indies.

The extraordinary grace and lightness of the freestanding staircase in the main hallway of the Thomas Ruggles House, Columbia Falls, Maine, have caused admiring comment for decades. Visually impressive, it is hardly a miracle of carpentry, since the strong crossbeam at the landing is capable of carrying a very heavy load. Wood was the obvious material for buildings in the early days of the republic—timber was plentiful, particularly in Maine, where for four months each winter, woodsmen lived in the forest, cut pine logs, skidded them over the snow by ox and horse sled, and piled them by the riverbank. When the river ice broke up, the logs were tumbled into the water to be carried in spectacular confusion to downstream sawmills near the seaports. Lumber was Maine's principal export in the eighteenth and nineteenth centuries, and the great river valleys connecting forest with sea were its lifelines of commerce.

The staircase in the Ruggles House displays exquisite wood-working and carving. The skills of the country carpenter, who could shape wood into a great variety of structural members by simple hand-and-tool techniques, were nearly universal among able-bodied men who worked with their hands. The introduction of nail- and spike-cutting machines after 1790 and of the power-driven circular saw in 1814 greatly increased the production of boards and heavy timbers. But traditional handicraft techniques were sufficient to build the country's largest mills and bridges in addition to houses like that of Thomas Ruggles. The heavy New England frame of posts, girders, beams, and joists could be elaborated and enlarged to provide the structural basis for a great diversity of buildings—mills, warehouses, railroad stations, stores, and office blocks.

View from the parlor, across the central hallway, into the dining room of the Ruggles House. When the house was built, Maine was looking toward a future that seemed bright indeed. In 1808, even before statehood, *The American Encyclopedia* declared, "Of all the northern quarters of the Union, Maine is that which will increase the fastest." Maine's population of about 200,000 was being augmented rapidly by the incredible postrevolutionary immigration from Massachusetts and New Hampshire. Timber fever, cramped spaces to the south, and plain restlessness all brought emigrants to Maine's coast.

The chimney piece's colonnettes and inset panels in the parlor of the Ruggles House are in natural mahogany surrounded by off-white painted woodwork of delicate design. The meticulous wood carving on both the exterior and interior of the house was probably executed by the builder, Aaron Simmons Sherman, who also built the meetinghouse and the large Nathan Buchnam House

in the village. The looking glass between the windows, with a lyre motif in its crest, is original to the house. The lyre is also evident in the backs of the two armchairs in the room, which also belonged to the Ruggles family. Unlike most houses of this type, the Ruggles House is rectangular, not square, in plan, and only one room deep.

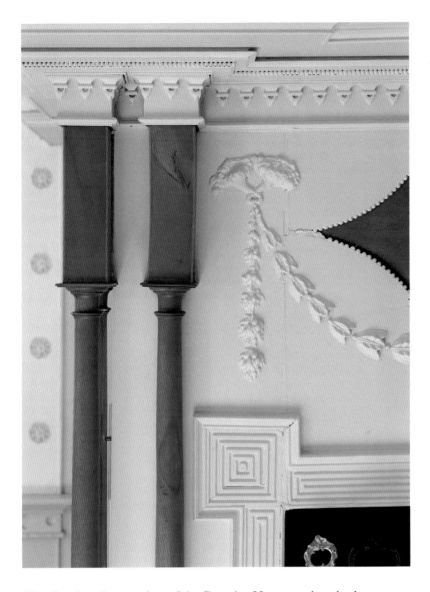

The fine interior carving of the Ruggles House makes the house an important architectural landmark. Aaron Simmons Sherman came from Marshfield, Massachusetts, with a fine reputation, and the Ruggles House, built in the small village of Columbia Falls in the remote wilderness of Maine, was his unquestioned masterpiece. Ruggles was the most important man in town, and money was apparently no object; architectural distinction seems to have been the goal of both owner and builder. In 1820, the part of the Massachusetts coast that became the state of Maine was a heavily wooded land, sparsely settled by hardy pioneers who established fisheries or engaged in the fur trade. But it was the forest that offered golden opportunities to energetic early settlers like Ruggles.

The country Empire desk in the west bedchamber of the Ruggles House, Columbia Falls, Maine, was originally a Ruggles family possession. The desk was given to a neighbor in the nineteenth century; it was returned when the house was being restored.

The four-post bed with its arched canopy, the comb-back Windsor chair, and the small spinning wheel in the west bedchamber of the Ruggles House are all family pieces. Judge Ruggles had little time to enjoy his beautiful house; he died in 1820, shortly after it was completed, while holding court in Machias. The house became the home of an unknown number of Ruggles children and descendants in the ensuing generations. As the family fortune ebbed away, the house fell into disrepair. In the early 1900s remaining members of the Ruggles family decided to save the old house. Most prominent

among them was Mary Ruggles Chandler, the first registered woman pharmacist in Maine and an inspiring example of New England womanhood. With relatives and friends, she formed the Ruggles Historical Society in 1921 and sought the advice and guidance of William Sumner Appleton, founder of the Society for the Preservation of New England Antiquities. Appleton, a vigorous defender of old houses, persuasively recommended that the Ruggles House be restored, suitably furnished, and opened as a house museum.

preceding page
The Lady Pepperrell House, Kittery Point, Maine, was built in 1760 for Lady Mary Pepperrell, widow of Sir William Pepperrell, the hero of the Louisbourg Expedition of 1745. The house is the most elaborate pre-Revolutionary Georgian-style residence in Maine and features a hipped roof and five-bay facade, a central pavilion with a triangular pediment, dentils, and Ionic pilasters, and a doorway embellished with consoles supporting a horizontal pediment. The Lady Pepperrell House has other features common to substantial houses of the period: a low-pitched hipped roof without balustrade or dormers, quoins instead of pilasters on the outside corners of the principal facade, flushboard siding instead of clapboards on the pavilion, and four exterior wall chimneys instead of two interior chimneys. Clearly one of the finest examples of Georgian design in the Piscataqua River basin, the Lady Pepperrell House captured the attention of architects in the colonial revival period.

opposite page
The Lady Pepperrell House contains much fine Georgian woodwork and is similar in many respects to the Vassall-Craigie-Longfellow House in Cambridge, Massachusetts, although the architect remains unknown. The openwork newel post, carved from the block, is typical of the work of ship carvers along the seacoast. The pillar-and-arch wallpaper is a reproduction of an English wallpaper of 1760–70, copied from an original sample found in the Paul Revere House in Boston.

following pages
The doorway connection between the front and back stair halls on the upper landing of the Lady Pepperrell House is similar to the arrangement found in the Vassall-Craigie-Longfellow House in Cambridge, Massachusetts. The house passed through a number of owners' hands after Lady Pepperrell's death in 1789, but only a few changes were made to the structure. By 1874 its occupant, Sally Cutts, had allowed the building to fall into disrepair. When Oliver Cutts acquired the property, he made numerous necessary repairs, replaced the windows with two-over-two double-hung sashes, added a second story to the ell, and gave the exterior a polychromatic paint scheme. William M. Wood III of Piqua, Ohio, purchased the house in this condition in 1922 and engaged John Mead Howells, New York architect and Kittery summer resident, to restore the house.

The paint colors of the North Drawing Room of the Lady Pepperrell House, including the pink doors and window shutters, are based on paint analysis. The wallpaper reproduces the original English pattern of about 1760, a sample of which is still on the walls. About the time that the Pepperrell House was built, Kittery and the other older towns of southern New Hampshire and coastal Maine were advancing toward economic maturity, shifting from fishing and lumbering to diversified agriculture. Not only did farming promise permanent self-sufficiency for most towns of the region, but the shift to a basically agricultural economy produced social changes viewed by the sober-minded as vast improvements. Farming demanded a regimen of hard work, it fostered an attachment to property, it encouraged close family life, it required the development of varied handicraft skills, and it served as a nursery for the Puritan virtues of thrift, sobriety, and diligence.

The dining room of the Lady Pepperrell House is enlivened by
the black and white painted diamond pattern of the floor, which
reproduces the original decorative treatment.

Where rivers were short and drainage or catchment basins small and near tidewater, the supply of waterpower soon reached its limits and windmills appeared, such as this one in Jamestown, Rhode Island. In early colonial gristmills, power by wind or water was geared to drive a single pair of stones—the runner stone and the bedstone. The millstones were grooved or "furrowed" in a pattern that caused the meal to flow away from the centers of the stones to their circumferences. Many sources of native rock were used to produce millstones in colonial America, including granite from the well-known quarries at Westerly, Rhode Island.

opposite page

The Eleazer Arnold House in Lincoln, Rhode Island, begun in 1687 and raised to two stories in 1800, is a typical Rhode Island "stone-ender," leaving the masonry exposed; the massive chimney is a fine example of the pilastered type. In seventeenth-century New England houses, materials were for the most part left in their natural state, with all structural elements exposed. The seventeenth-century builder was an artisan, not a professional architect; working within limited technical means, he was simply carrying on the traditional ideas and structural methods that had been passed down since the Middle Ages. It was from the natural beauty of materials—wood, stone, and brick—that he enjoyed the greatest aesthetic enrichment.

In the seventeenth and early eighteenth centuries, Wethersfield, Connecticut—a river port forty miles from Long Island Sound— was the center of commerce for the entire Connecticut River valley. In the 1630s, the river formed an excellent natural harbor at what is now Wethersfield Cove. Between 1661 and 1699 six or seven warehouses for the coastal and West Indies trade were built in this area; the Cove Warehouse is the only one that still stands. About 1700 the course of the river altered considerably, and the natural harbor became a cove unsuitable as an anchorage. The Cove Warehouse, built of oak and sheathed with pine in the 1690s, served Wethersfield's shipping interests for many years. From Wethersfield the Connecticut River valley farmers exported grains, cattle, horses, hides, flaxseed, dried fish, pork, and beef, as well as Windsor's tobacco and Wethersfield's red onions. The returning ships brought salt, sugar, molasses, rum, tea, coffee, and spices. By the middle of the eighteenth century luxuries of considerable sophistication—fine fabrics, ceramics and glass, cutlery, books, even children's toys—were imported and sold in Wethersfield.

Isaac Stevens, a saddler born in 1755 in Glastonbury, is survived by little besides his account book and the house he built in 1788–89 in Wethersfield, Connecticut. The fine dentil molding of the cornice and subdued but definite shaping of the upper door casing lift this facade well above the ordinary. The house is typical Connecticut Georgian in plan, perpetuating the late-colonial tradition. It was brought up-to-date a generation or so after it was built, probably for the marriage of Stevens's daughter Sally. At that time the parlor was given a fine dentil cornice and a mantel with attenuated pilasters.

The Hoyt-Barnum House in Stamford, Connecticut, built by
Samuel Hait (Hoyt) in 1699, is the oldest surviving structure in
downtown Stamford. The simple structure is an interesting study
in both early construction and the evolution of a building, as each
successive occupant has made personal additions or adaptations
to the house.

The Buttolph-Williams House in Wethersfield, Connecticut, was built about 1692 and occupied first by David Buttolph and then, in the eighteenth century, by Daniel Williams.

The fireplace surround in the whitewashed south chamber of the Buttolph-Williams House is painted the original red.
One of the two handsome banister-back armchairs, about 1710, has Spanish feet.

View through the second-floor landing into the hall chamber of the Buttolph-Williams House. The door in the plank wall opens to the attic stairs. In the hall chamber, the day bed is upholstered in woven flame stitch fabric; the English looking glass is surrounded by a wide border of late-seventeenth-century stump work.

preceding pages

The table to the left of the fireplace in the parlor of the John Deming House, Wethersfield, Connecticut, is a net table, once owned by Daniel Buck (1744–1808), which was used by the Buck family to cast on 150 feet of seine fishing net. When the French traveler Brissot de Warville visited Connecticut in 1788, he reported: "Wethersfield is remarkable for its immense fields of onions, which are exported in prodigious quantities to the West Indies, and for its elegant meetinghouse. They say that every Sunday an enchanting spectacle is offered by the numerous pretty girls who gather here and by the pleasant music with which the divine service is interspersed."

opposite page

View of the John Deming House in Wethersfield, Connecticut, built about 1667. The Buck family, related to the original Deming owners, have lived in the house since 1837. In 1634, at a deep bend in the Connecticut River, John Oldham and nine other settlers founded Wethersfield. Marsh hay in the low meadows and the rich alluvial soil soon attracted others, who planted their farms on the broad terrace above the river. The surrounding forest provided timber for houses, and the town was laid out with a common alongside the present cove. At that time the town of Wethersfield included Rocky Hill to the south, Newington to the west, and Glastonbury across the river to the east, where settlers pastured their livestock. Roads and turnpikes soon connected farmers with merchants and markets beyond the town, and locally built vessels carried farm, forest, and fishery products to New York, Barbados, and beyond.

In the corner of the kitchen of the Silas Deane House, Wethersfield, Connecticut, to the right of the fireplace, is a brownstone sink. The large maple-and-pine stretcher table with breadboard top, made in New England about 1730, was originally painted red. The kitchen equipment includes early wooden and pewter bowls, pottery, home-spun cloths, and a brass-and-iron clock jack of about 1730.

The Silas Deane House, built in 1766, is architecturally unusual for its time and location. Instead of the typical central-hall, four-over-four arrangement, it has an off-center doorway and a very wide entrance hall, and the interior gives an impression of great spaciousness. The paneling of the elegant front parlor is original, as is the fireplace surround, finely carved of brownstone from Portland, Connecticut. The Rhode Island mahogany chairs, are from a set of twelve made about 1770. China trade porcelain is set on the Philadelphia Chippendale tripod table of about 1765. The mahogany fire screen, probably English, about 1750, is fitted with a needlework panel of later date. The portrait of Silas Deane, painted about 1766, is attributed to William Johnston.

At the beginning of the eighteenth century, the Bates family received and settled on grants of land along the Mill River in the center of Stamford and in the eastern wilderness near the Norwalk line. John Bates joined his uncle Jonathan in homesteading in the woods on the outskirts of Stamford; he was married in 1718, lived on this land in 1736, and died in 1759, leaving nine children. The salt-box house of the Bates-Scofield Homestead in Darien, Connecticut, was built by John Bates about 1736 around a massive chimney stack, which measures nine by ten feet at its base.

Thomas Griswold III of the Nut Plains District built this classic salt-box in Guilford, Connecticut, about 1774 for his two sons, Ezra and John, on a commanding knoll along a picturesque stretch of the Card Post Road. It was a two-family dwelling until 1805, when Griswold's son John sold his interest in the property; four more generations of the family lived in the house. Today the dwelling serves as a house museum reflecting the material culture and social life of the late eighteenth and early nineteenth centuries, as well as the headquarters of the Guilford Keeping Society.

The red wool-flock wallpaper in the bedchamber of the Joseph Webb House, Wethersfield, Connecticut, with a large-scale rococo leaf design, was hung for the occasion of George Washington's visit in May 1781. The foot post is part of the Philadelphia Chippendale mahogany bed, about 1780. In 1915 Wallace Nutting acquired the Webb House and between 1916 and 1918 he photographed fashionable Wethersfield ladies there; he was forced by financial difficulties to put the Webb House on the market in 1919.

opposite page
George Washington slept in this bedchamber at the Webb House in May 1781. The easy chair, New England, about 1780, was originally owned by the Webb family.

opposite page

The Clark-Haskell House in Lisbon, in southeastern Connecticut, was built in 1796; the date is cut into one of the chimney stones. The main house and a modern ell were added onto a small house on the site, probably built in the 1740s, which is now the keeping room. The floor plan and sturdy construction of the main house embody the conservatism and provincial awkwardness of Connecticut. Directly inside the front door, narrow stairs ascend to the bedrooms on the second floor. On the ground floor a central chimney serves the dining room to the left of the stairs, the front parlor to the right of the stairs, and the back parlor behind them, which extends the length of the house in the manner of the long room found under the lean-to of salt-box houses. The house is encircled by a full cornice, and the projecting central pavilion and giant pilasters give the plain, clapboarded facade a certain monumentality. In spite of its fundamentally Palladian character, the exterior of the house has Federal elements such as the delicate moldings surrounding the elegant fanlight over the front door and those around the Palladian window above it.

This New England painted pine corner cupboard of about 1800 is in the back parlor of the Clark-Haskell House. In addition to three reticulated Worcester porcelain fruit baskets of about 1760, the cupboard contains a delightful and varied assortment of English ceramics from Staffordshire and Leeds, delftware, creamware, and Chinese export porcelain.

preceding pages

The cherry block-front chest on chest in the back parlor of the Clark-Haskell House was made in Colchester, Connecticut, about 1780. Its distinctive regional variations include the broken-scroll pediment with dentils and a shell pendant below the central finial. The cherry drop-leaf table in the corner and the small painted maple tea table in the foreground were both made in New England about 1750. The turned and painted banister-back Connecticut armchairs date from around 1720.

opposite page

The engaged, fluted quarter column in the corner of the front parlor of the Clark-Haskell House conceals a structural beam. The mahogany desk-and-bookcase was made in Massachusetts, 1760–80, and has finely carved finials, rosettes, and foliage on the bonnet, engaged pilasters on the upper section, and leaf-carved bracket feet. Displayed in it is a collection of miniature Chinese porcelains, English pottery, and jade. The walnut side chair, once in the collection of Howard Reifsnyder, was made in Philadelphia, 1740–60. Above the Philadelphia walnut armchair, 1760–80, is a portrait of Reeve Lewis painted in 1808 by Thomas Sully. Sully's contemporaneous pendant portrait of Lewis's wife, Rachel Waln Thomas, is reflected in the mirrored door of the bookcase. The mahogany tea table was made in Rhode Island about 1750–70.

Between the windows in a bedroom in the Clark-Haskell House is a pine wall cupboard made in New England in the eighteenth century. On top of it is a set of Irish pewter haystack, or harvester's, measures, and on the shelves are English ceramics and American pewter plates and porringers. The mid-eighteenth-century marbleized table is from New England. The portrait of an unidentified girl, attributed to Mary B. Tucker, dates from the first half of the nineteenth century. On the early-eighteenth-century painted chest of drawers is a grain-painted miniature dower chest made in New England in the early nineteenth century. The painted maple bed partially visible at the right is one of a pair made in New England about 1800.

The mahogany tester bed in a bedroom in the Clark-Haskell House
has swelled, reeded foot posts; it was made in New England about
1810. The cherry side chair between the windows was made in
Connecticut about 1780; above it hangs a portrait of an
unidentified woman attributed to the early-nineteenth-century
Prior-Hamblin (or Hamblen) group. The mahogany miniature
dressing mirror at the left was made in New York about 1820.

The Samuel Read Hall House, Brownington, Vermont, was built in 1832 for George Carlton West, a young lawyer originally from St. Johnsbury, Vermont. West had practiced law in Norwich, Vermont, before coming to Brownington in 1822. Much of this picturesque section of rural Vermont, known as the Northeast Kingdom, was not settled until after the Revolutionary War, when land was offered to veterans of the war who, it was hoped, would provide a measure of security and stability to the area. Many of the other early families in Brownington came from southern New Hampshire. Samuel Read Hall, founder of the local school, lived in the house between 1856 and 1877.

following page
Above a collection of kitchen utensils in the Samuel Read Hall House hangs a nineteenth-century cheese basket. Vermont is a demanding state to live in, and early Vermonters had to be frugal, resourceful, and ingenious. Their versatility is as noteworthy as their self-sufficiency; Vermont women, as described in a nineteenth-century gazetteer, "picked their own wool, carded their own rolls, spun their own yarn, drove their own looms, made their own cloth, cut, made, and mended their own garments, dipped their own candles, made their own soap, bottomed their own chairs, braided their own baskets, wove their own carpets, quilts, and coverlets, picked their own geese, milked their own cows, fed their own calves, and went visiting or to meetings on their own feet."

THE MIDDLE COLONIES: FROM SETTLEMENT TO INDEPENDENCE

The Dutch in New York:

Rough and Unrestrained

One hundred years before New Netherland was founded as a permanent settlement, Giovanni da Verrazano, an Italian navigator working for King Francis I of France, came upon a remarkable natural harbor and the broad river that flowed into it. Verrazano reported to the king: "We found a pleasant situation among some little steep hills, through which a very large river forced its way to the sea." Continuing to search for a passage to the Orient, Verrazano sailed east along the south shore of Long Island "greatly regretting to leave this region," which, he wrote, "seemed so commodious and delightful, and which we supposed must contain great riches." But the narrows that now bear his name did not lead to China, disappointing Francis I as much as Verrazano, and the French did nothing to consolidate the discovery.

Almost a century later, the Dutch East India Company, looking for a direct and safe route to India, hired the English mariner Henry Hudson to search for a northeast passage. In 1609 Hudson guided his high-pooped ship upstream to a point near present-day Albany, but no permanent settlement was made until 1624, when the newly formed Dutch West India Company founded New Netherland and sent settlers to Fort Orange (near Albany). Following a harsh winter and faced with the threat of attacks by local Indians, the Fort Orange settlers joined newly arrived Dutch settlers in New Amsterdam, at the southern tip of Manhattan. With an excellent natural harbor and access, via the Hudson River, to the fertile farmland of western New York and the upstate fur trade, the settlement had great commercial potential and soon became the heart of New Netherland.

The Dutch West India Company erected a fort in new Amsterdam in 1625; within its walls were the governor's house, a double-gabled church with a squat tower, a prison, barracks, and gallows, and the office of the company. Outside, the company engineer laid out "bouweries," or farms, along the waterfront.

Within twenty-five years, the Dutch settlement was a bustling, if unruly town, boasting a public mill, a shipbuilding industry, several sizable farms, and several taverns. The town had 1,000 people in 1650, and its population would more than double during the following decade. When the English captured the city from Governor Peter Stuyvesant in September 1664, they found a town of several hundred houses south of present-day Wall Street, where a palisade had been erected in 1653 to ward off attacks by Indians and the English. There were also several other small settlements on Manhattan and around the bay; Brooklyn, for example, was a tiny village dating from 1646.

New Amsterdam soon outgrew its status as a fur trading post. By the end of the Dutch period, the settlement, with its waterfront, curving streets, and gabled skyline, had become a miniature Amsterdam. The important merchants formed a burgher aristocracy and asserted political leadership similar to that which dominated the cities of Holland. Spacious fruit orchards and tulip gardens lay behind the houses of the wealthier merchants. More numerous than these merchants were the middle class: tavern keepers, petty traders, doctors, surveyors, accountants, and shopkeepers. Artisans of every description drifted to Manhattan Island—smiths, sailmakers, cabinetmakers, shoemakers, and carpenters. The imported artisans constructed large brick houses for the merchants, with roofs of red and black pantiles and quaint stepped or straight-line gable ends. Below the merchants and artisans in income and status were common laborers and those, black and white, who attended to the personal wants of their masters. The population was heterogeneous from the outset: in 1664 the Dutch formed about two-thirds of the population and the British most of the remainder, while Germans, Jews, French, Finns, Swedes, and blacks, both slaves and free, were also present in smaller numbers. Governor William Kieft told the Father Jogues in 1644 that eighteen languages were spoken at the colony, and the worthy Jesuit observed that Manhattan had already acquired the "arrogance of Babel."

Religion played a less important role in the lives of the citizens of New Netherland than in either Roman Catholic Quebec or Puritan New England. From the colony's beginning, the Dutch sought profits rather than the conversion of the Indians or the establishment of a wilderness Zion ruled by God's elect. The colony's settlers, reflecting this secular spirit, were often unruly characters, notorious for their addiction to strong drink. One visitor, the pastor Michaëlius, observed that the residents were "for the most part . . . rather rough and unrestrained." While the Protestant Netherlands had been a haven for persecuted religious groups during the seventeenth century, and even though the Dutch West India Company, reflecting this tolerant spirit, urged their officials to welcome newcomers and minimize religious persecution, Governor Stuyvesant regarded nonconformists as potential rebels: he expelled Quakers, discouraged the immigration of Jews, and blocked the formal organization of a Lutheran church. However, tolerant outsiders eventually prevailed, and the Flushing Remonstrance of 1657 guaranteed settlers "liberty of Conscience, according to the custome and manner of Holland, without molestation or disturbance"; this bold assertion foreshadowed New York's great tradition of religious freedom and acceptance.

The Dutch remained a strong presence in anglicized New York long after 1664. Dutch enclaves in Ulster County, northern New Jersey, and western Long Island clung to the language until the early years of the nineteenth century, and place names such as Harlem, Brooklyn, and Kinderhook, common words such as boss, stoop, and cruller, and political figures with names like Van Buren and Roosevelt kept alive the heritage of New Netherland. The Dutch colony had developed a more "American" culture than any other group of colonists in their part of the world. Modern Americans can see in these early New Yorkers some of their most cherished characteristics—a commercial spirit, a keen interest in material things, a zest for life, and a tolerant attitude toward people of varying religious and racial backgrounds.

New York, An English Province:
Conveniently Situated for Trade

The Duke of York, unrestricted by any popular assembly, ruled New York for twenty-one years as duke and for three years as king in the pattern of arbitrary government established by the Dutch West India Company. His primary concern in New York was financial—he controlled the trade of the colony, fixed taxes, granted land, and directed the defense. But for all its diversity and its British leadership, the colony was unmistakably Dutch. As English colonists arrived, New York gradually turned English, but not with a rush.

The first English governor, Richard Nicholls, proved to be successful not only in appeasing the Dutch but also in establishing proprietary rule without stirring an English revolt, by promising the city's important merchants that New York would "bloom and grow like the Cedars of Lebanon." Of blooming and growing there was precious little for a time, since trade with the Netherlands was stopped and the increase in trade with England was much less than the New York merchants had anticipated. But trade did develop, and New York City soon became the hub for dealings throughout the region. The leading New York families—Van Cortlandt, Bayard, Van Rensselaer, Stuyvesant, Livingston, Beekman, and Morriss—sold wheat to Boston and furs to Europe. New York imported rum and molasses from the West Indies, wines from Madeira, and "Indian goods"—blankets, woolens, guns, gunpowder, and lead, the commodities the Indians wanted in exchange for their furs—from Europe. New York City was given a formal monopoly on export trade and on the processing of flour for export, irritating processors upstate.

These economic irritations increased, and by 1688 merchants outside the city were ready to revolt. Country farmers and millers resented the monopoly granted to flour bolters in New York City and Albany; seaports on eastern Long Island complained that regulations requiring them to funnel all their trade through New York City were ruining their business with Boston and the West Indies; and Albany fur traders deeply resented that their cargoes had to be reshipped for Europe from the port of New York. The deteriorating economic situation caused by the founding of

Pennsylvania in 1681 intensified these grievances. Philadelphia merchants captured a large portion of the trade of New Jersey, gained control of the fur trade along the Delaware River, and diverted much of the tobacco trade from New York shippers.

The political situation, reflecting both colonial and European tensions, was also reaching a boiling point. Rumors spread through New York in 1688 that Governor Thomas Dongan and James II, both Roman Catholics, were hatching a plot to restore Catholic power in New York. Tensions with the French over the Iroquois and the western fur trade convinced many citizens that the French might invade New York as part of a Catholic conspiracy to destroy Protestantism in New York; the revocation of the Edict of Nantes in France in 1685 made them particularly wary of the French. New Yorkers of Dutch descent recalled the religious persecution and suffering their ancestors endured during the rule of the Spanish Duke of Alva, so when James II was dethroned in the Glorious Revolution of 1688 and Governor Edmund Andros was imprisoned in Boston by the colonials, Jacob Leisler, a wealthy merchant supported by Dutch artisans, laborers, and merchants, seized control of the city in the name of William of Orange. His two-year rebellion was opposed strenuously by wealthy English and Dutch merchants, and he was eventually arrested and executed for treason.

New York's early settlement had flowed up the Hudson River valley from New York City, reaching Albany, a frontier trading post, and Schenectady on the Mohawk, the furthest outpost of the colony. A second seaborne settlement wave had crossed Long Island Sound from New Haven and Connecticut into Long Island, and some settlers had come overland from New Haven into Westchester County. The interior counties of Dutchess, Ulster, Orange, and Albany were Dutch strongholds; in Albany they constituted 93 percent of the population. Besides Dutch, English, and New Englanders, French Huguenots had arrived in New York in 1685 and German Palatines in 1710. This melting pot pattern was even more pronounced in New York City, resulting in a great mixture of nationalities and religious sects, although English influence began to predominate after about 1700. The growing population of upriver counties, including Westchester, Ulster, and Albany, began to organize into New England–style towns, while religious sects like the Quakers formed small, exclusive communities. Another, more unusual unit of local authority was the manor, granted after 1691 by the governor in order to build a political following among large landholders.

Culturally, New York City lagged behind Boston and Philadelphia throughout the colonial period. The *American Gazetteer* of 1762 complained about New York: "Through a long shameful neglect of all the arts and sciences, the common speech is extremely corrupt, and the evidences of a bad taste, both as to thought and language, are visible in their proceedings public and private. There is nothing the ladies so generally neglect as reading and indeed all the arts for the improvement of the mind—a neglect in which the men have set the example." A majority of the children of colonial New York never saw the inside of a schoolhouse, and the favored minority received little more than an introduction to reading, writing, and arithmetic. A few wealthy families hired tutors, but the middle class and gentry usually sent their children to masters who set up private schools. John Sharpe, the chaplain of the King's forces, reported in 1713: "The City is so conveniently Situated for Trade and the Genius of the people are so inclined to merchandise that they generally seek no other Education for their children than writing and Arithmetick." A few sons of the aristocracy attended Oxford and Cambridge, and in the New World, Yale was for many years the favorite and most convenient college for New Yorkers. But its orthodox Calvinism irked both "New Light" Presbyterians and Anglicans, and they accordingly established King's College in 1754 (later Columbia University) and made it a center of Anglican and Loyalist sentiment.

The elite followed the latest fashions of London in their house furnishings, clothing, and amusements as well as in music, painting, literature, and architecture. In the 1750s, William Tuckey, organist and concert master, gave many concerts with his choir at Trinity Church; wealthy merchants and landlords sought out portrait painters like Robert Feke, Benjamin West, and John Singleton Copley, and the New York *Gazette,* the fifth colonial newspaper and the first in New York, was founded in 1725 by William Bradford. The lifestyle was luxurious enough to evoke favorable comment by visitors from England and other colonies. The rich diverted themselves by riding, hunting, and boating; during the 1730s public balls and theater became fashionable. The life of the aristocratic minority was of course quite different from that of the farmers and middle class, not to mention mechanics, artisans, servants, and slaves. Though life could be grim for some New Yorkers, men of all classes found relaxation in the grog houses and flocked to the horse races and cockfights. Social life centered around the taverns, of which there was one for every fifty-five inhabitants of New York City in 1772. The larger taverns served as informal information centers, supplying newspapers from other cities and entertaining travelers from other colonies.

After 1664 the Dutch continued to build houses characterized by gables turned toward the street and handsome roofs that curved outward, forming an overhang beyond the wall. As they became more prosperous, the Dutch built larger houses, adopting such features as the two-pitched gambrel from New England and introducing Renaissance notes of decor in the interior trim. Anglo merchants built square brick Georgian houses with stone trimmings and triangular, semicircular, or broken pediments above the windows and doors. Other typical features were columns framing the doorways, fanlights, and balustraded roofs or simple gables with dormer windows.

The Confusion and Colonization of New Jersey:

A Quaker Commonwealth

Within a few months of receiving his charter for New Netherland in 1664, the Duke of York gave New Jersey to two close friends, Sir George Carteret and Lord John Berkeley, proprietors who were also involved in the Carolinas. At this point the area's population did not exceed two hundred. Interested exclusively in profits from land speculation, they soon realized that the colony would not yield any immediate returns and eventually sold their rights. Berkeley transferred his half-interest (West New Jersey) to two Quakers whose share by 1692 was held by forty-eight men; Carteret died in 1680, and his share (East New Jersey) eventually went to twenty-four owners. New Jersey land titles consequently became a nightmare of complexity.

With New York City dominating East Jersey's trade and Philadelphia controlling West Jersey's, the colony remained an economic backwater. New Jersey's politics were also hampered.

Berkeley and Carteret assumed, when the Duke granted them the land in 1664, that governmental power went with it. The Duke's failure to confirm or deny this led to continuing disputes with New York's governors. In 1702 the proprietors reached an agreement long enough to resign political control to the Crown, and New York's governor became New Jersey's as well.

In England, Quakers had been imprisoned and harassed after the Restoration, so the notion of America as a place of refuge and religious toleration was very attractive. Substantial migration of the Society of Friends to West New Jersey took place, and the colony became a "Quaker commonwealth" under promises contained in a set of "Concessions" issued in 1677. These embodied the usual terms offered by proprietors to settlers, including a legislative assembly, liberty of conscience, and a system of head rights for free settlers and servants. The Concessions also stipulated that jury trials be held in the accused's own neighborhood and banned imprisonment for debt, restrictions that came from the sect's own experience. The Concessions also guaranteed annual elections and secret balloting, enfranchised all male inhabitants, and set up a powerful legislature for West New Jersey. While attention to the legal rights of property owners was common in seventeenth-century political thought, the idea of human liberty for every man, irrespective of his status in the community, was not. Like William Penn's later "Frame of Government" for Pennsylvania, the Concessions testify to the extent to which the Quakers shared and contributed to the more radical political ideas of the late seventeenth century.

William Penn and His Holy Experiment:

A Greene Country Towne

If ever one man created a city, William Penn created Philadelphia. He named this capital city in advance (after the Greek word for brotherly love), chose the site, devised the street plan, and distributed the house lots. Young Penn wanted his city to be radically different from any other town in the Western world. His urban design was strikingly original, reflecting his tastes as an English landed gentleman and his ideals as a persecuted Quaker.

He remembered the bubonic plague in London in 1665 and the disastrous fire of 1666, and set out to create "a greene Country Towne, which will never be burnt, and allways be wholsome," an urban center that would not contaminate his holy experiment in Pennsylvania. As a Quaker, Penn envisioned a place of refuge for the persecuted, where the spiritual union of all Christians might be more than a dream; he intended to live at peace with the Indians, so he made no provision for city walls, fortifications, or garrisons of soldiers. Penn sought the friendship of neighboring governors, Indians in his territory, and those Europeans already settled there. He published several tracts describing the colony's advantages, circulated them in Britain, and translated them for distribution in Germany. His ideas had great appeal among German pietist sects, and they migrated in great numbers to Pennsylvania, where they became known as the Pennsylvania Germans.

Philadelphia was shaped by the hundreds of colonists who moved to the new settlement during the 1680s and 1690s, and very quickly Philadelphia developed into the third-largest port on the Atlantic seaboard, after Boston and New York. Immigration sharply stimulated colonial development: productivity expanded rapidly because of the enlarged labor force and increased market, and colonial merchants accumulated capital more readily. A heterogeneous mix of Quakers, Anglicans, Presbyterians, and Baptists was drawn to the town by Penn's policy of religious toleration; Pennsylvania's climate, topography, and soil resembled the Old World's, and the colony contained a seemingly limitless amount of cheap, fertile land. Beyond Pennsylvania stretched the Great Valley, leading southwest into Virginia and the Carolinas, offering even more fertile land and a highway into the continent's interior. And Penn's colony offered other advantages: no tax-supported church, an affinity between Quakers and German pietist sects, and peaceful Indian relations.

Before Penn started his city in 1681, there was nothing resembling a commercial town in the Delaware Valley. When Penn received his charter for Pennsylvania, the total European population trading and farming along the Delaware River—mostly Swedes and Finns, with a few Dutch and English—was less than 2,000. The settlement around Philadelphia grew rapidly: when Penn arrived late in 1682 to take up the governorship, he was pleased to see that the settlement already had some 4,000

inhabitants and contained eighty dwellings in Philadelphia alone. Penn soon announced that the Duke of York had sold him the three counties of Delaware—Newcastle, Kent, and Sussex—which were then annexed to Pennsylvania and subject to the new colony's laws and privileges. The inclusion of the three "Lower Counties," as they were then known, gave him adequate access to the sea and protected the approaches to the Delaware River and Philadelphia.

Shortly after obtaining his royal charter, Penn announced that he would lay out "a large Towne or Citty in the most Convenient place upon the River for health & Navigation." When he arrived in the colony, he decided to expand west from the Delaware to the Schuylkill: Philadelphia now stretched two miles from east to west between the two rivers, and one mile from north to south. The site had many natural advantages: Shielded by the Appalachians from extremes of weather, the city offered a varied but not severe climate. The Delaware provided a deep and commodious harbor; dozens of big ships could anchor close to shore, and there was a cove and a sandy beach for small boats. The Schuylkill River, despite its rapids, offered the best highway to the interior of Pennsylvania. Most important, Philadelphia was surrounded by what would soon become the richest agricultural hinterland of any colonial city. It lay at the center of a circle of splendid farm country that reached fifty miles or more in every direction, drawing New Jersey as well as Pennsylvania and Delaware into its orbit. The new settlers who poured into this region and cleared its forests in the late seventeenth and early eighteenth centuries not only produced commodities for Philadelphia merchants to export but also created a market for imported goods.

Penn's plan for a "great towne" was a 1,200-acre rectangular grid, providing far more generous city limits than any other early American town, with enough room for expansion to permit many years of orderly future growth. He offered the city's best building lots to the First Purchasers and other early settlers, but he reserved more than half the city lots for future sale or rental. Beyond the urban limits he set aside about 8,000 acres in what is now North and West Philadelphia as so-called liberty lands, where each purchaser of 5,000 acres of Pennsylvania land was entitled to a dividend of eighty acres. Keeping to his original idea of gentlemen farmers surrounding the commercial center, Penn expected the chief landowners in the colony to build their houses in a suburban belt, and the proprietor himself proposed to build a house at Fairmount near the present Philadelphia Art Museum, overlooking the Schuylkill. Thomas Holme advertised the layout of the new city in his famous plat, *Portraiture of the City of Philadelphia,* published in London in 1683, displaying Penn's symmetrical pattern of wide streets intersecting large squares. Market and Broad Streets were (and are) 100 feet wide, broader than the widest thoroughfares in seventeenth-century London; most other streets were fifty feet wide, with the east-west streets named after local trees and the cross streets numbered, in keeping with Penn's taste for simplicity and order. Four large squares were set aside to be parks open to all. At the intersection of High and Broad Streets, where City Hall now stands, Penn designated a central square of ten acres to be bordered by the principal public buildings, such as the Quaker meetinghouse, the state house, the market house, and the schoolhouse. Despite the two riverfronts, Penn's city had an inward-facing design, focusing on this central square.

During its first two decades Philadelphia grew rapidly, from a few hundred inhabitants in 1683 to over 2,000 in 1700; it was still a very small place, but it was already one of the three or four biggest towns in British North America, almost as populous as New York. At this point the town was a raw frontier community. Pigs and goats ran freely through the avenues, enticed by plentiful garbage, and the very heart of the town was an undrained sewer. The town's first houses were built of logs, Swedish style, the earlier Scandinavian settlers teaching the English newcomers how to notch and fit the wood together without using nails. Soon, however, English colonists returned to their native building habits of wood frame and brick construction. By 1690 there was enough brick construction to occupy four brick makers and ten bricklayers.

Structural Innovation Begins:

Many Brave Brick Houses

In plan and materials, the buildings of the Middle Colonies reflected new conditions, and they showed the imagination and freedom with which the colonists attacked new problems. By and large, all of the colonists on the Atlantic seaboard were familiar with one or more of the then standard structural systems—wood frame, brick, and stone masonry. Wood was to become America's principal building material, far outstripping all others in its scope and versatility. Though the English brought with them the rudiments of our modern wood-framing systems, they were crude and inexact, left over from a feudal England still largely built of wood. These English wood frames proved to be unsuited to the colony's climate, whose violent and abrupt changes caused rapid expansion and contraction, cracking walls and reducing their efficiency. The colonists soon modified their structural systems to meet their new environment, covering the brick nogging with which the English had filled in the wood skeleton with two relatively impervious skins—a clapboard exterior and a plaster interior.

Since wood was both the most abundant and easily worked material, and the settlers were thoroughly familiar with it, it is not surprising that they adopted it as their favorite building material. In the succeeding decades, a giant lumber industry would arise from these beginnings, spurred on by the appearance of the steam-powered sawmill at the end of the eighteenth century. Much the same thing happened in brick manufacture. Although uncut stone was widely used in some parts of the colonies, it never became a real competitor of brick. The brick's small size, standardized production, and general availability made it the preeminent masonry material. As early as 1630, bricks were being commercially produced at Powder Horn Hill near Chelsea, Massachusetts. Even earlier, in 1611, Sir Thomas Dale had landed in Jamestown and immediately started "many essential improvements" which included a brickyard and a smith's forge; later the same year the colonial secretary reported that Henrico (near the present site of Richmond) boasted "three streets of well-framed houses, a handsome church, and the foundations for a more stately one laid in bricks."

Faced with empty building lots in 1683, Penn encouraged tradesmen and craftsmen to move into the city as soon as they signed an agreement to buy country land when financially able, with the proviso that they would immediately clear their town tract and start construction. In this manner he soon acquired a fair number of skilled artisans. He was especially interested in brick manufacture, and in November of that year granted to George Guest, a former whitesmith from West Jersey, two acres of land "to make Bricks on where he with his men hath begun to work by the

Swamp." Before local manufacture, all brick shipments came from England. To Robert Turner, who came to Philadelphia in 1683 with his family and seventeen servants, went the distinction of having the first all-brick home. In 1685 he estimated six hundred houses in Philadelphia, and "since I built my Brick House . . . many take example, and some that built Wooden Houses, are sorry for it: Brick building is said to be as cheap: Bricks are exceeding good, and better than when I built: More Makers fallen in, and Brick cheaper . . . and now many brave Brick Houses are going up, with good Cellars . . . Arthur Cook is building him a brave Brick House . . . William Frampton hath since built a good Brick house, by his Brew house and Bake house, and let the other for an Ordinary. John Wheeler, from New England, is building a good Brick house, by the Blew Anchor . . . I am Building another Brick house by mine, which is three large Stories high, besides a good large Brick Cellar under it, of two Bricks and a half thickness in the wall."

The majority of artisans arriving in Philadelphia during the 1680s were British-born and schooled in the London craft tradition. The rebuilding of London after the Great Fire of 1666 had provided temporary prosperity for all the building trades, but a bust eventually followed this boom, and by the 1680s a stifling depression had settled over the industry. In an unrestrained and glutted market, conditions were ripe for young men of ambition to make their way to the new colony in America, where William Penn promised that all sorts of craftsmen would be in demand. For Penn and the future of his venture in America, the economic distress of London builders was a happy coincidence. Philadelphia developed so rapidly in part because, from its beginnings, the town had a relatively large cadre of skilled artisans from all the basic building trades who, by one means or another, found themselves a place in Pennsylvania.

The English mathematician Joseph Moxon, who published his *Mechanick Exercises: or the Doctrine of Handy-works* (1678) on the eve of the founding of Pennsylvania, intended to delineate the basic tools and techniques employed in several manual crafts. His book provides a close, practical look at the work of joiners, carpenters, and bricklayers, and gives insight into the working relationships of the various building crafts. Moxon traces the step-by-step method for building a house in the late seventeenth century, a process dominated by the master builder, or master carpenter, who was

responsible for the entire fabric of a house and subcontracted the brickwork, joinery, glazing, plastering, and painting. General demands of size and site would be conveyed "on a single piece of Paper, describe the whole Building, as it shall appear to the Eye," to the master workman who would lay out the ground plan, interior partitions, major structural members, trim, and ornaments on a "draft" rendered to scale from every side. (How common such drafts were in colonial Philadelphia is difficult to know.) "Having drawn the draft" and secured approval, the carpenter had the cellar excavated; "then are the Cellar-Walls to be brought up by a Brick-layer" to ground level, or, if the house was to be entirely of brick, to lay all the walls. With the window frames in place, the glazier and plasterers were called in by the master workman and the interior and exterior trim completed by the carpenters, or, if the house was to be more embellished, joiners, carvers, painters, and marble workers were engaged. But it was the master carpenter who was the key person from design through delivery; the ultimate form and, especially, the final details were the result of his knowledge and skill.

With the focus of Philadelphia's first inhabitants on money-making, Penn's design for the city was quickly altered. During the 1680s and 1690s residents clustered as close to the Delaware as possible, refusing to spread out from river to river in accord with Penn's original scheme. By 1700 the Schuylkill side of the town was vacant, or virtually so, and on the Delaware side practically everyone lived within three or four blocks of the river—on much smaller, narrower, and more congested lots than Penn intended. Philadelphia was now nearly as large as New York City and closely rivaled it in trade and riches. In 1697 Penn estimated the city had 1,500 houses, and a combined town and country population of about 12,000. During the first quarter of the eighteenth century, Philadelphia gradually emerged from under the economic shadow of New York and Boston and carved out its own place in the trade pattern of the empire.

Forces of Continuity and Change in a Mercantile World:

Eight Hundred Important Merchants

Over time the colonists built an American society, a slow process of Americanization that took place during the years from the founding of colonies through the Revolution. They were people firmly committed to the New World, intent on staying and making their lives in America. For the most part they were ambitious, acquisitive men and women who had achieved a modicum of success in England and were attracted to the New World by the lure of greater success. Their intention in America was to better their lot in the world and, because it would contribute to their own betterment, to better the New World itself. This desire for improvement did not necessarily include a desire for broad changes in the English way of life; on the contrary, the early settler immediately set about reconstructing everything he had known in England—the only change desired being that he himself be endowed with a little more of the world's goods—and always insisted that he was an Englishman through and through. What the colonists knew in England about law, government, defense, marriage, land tenure, agriculture, and religion crossed the ocean with them, along with their tools and clothes and weapons. Just as they began breaking the American soil with an English plow, grubbing weeds with an English hoe, clothing themselves in English woolens, and lighting their houses with English candles, so they began to erect English institutions.

Colonization and the transformation of Englishmen into something other than English took place in a mercantile world. Cities like Philadelphia depended on trade and grew because they were convenient places for the exchange of goods. Other factors, such as a city's proximity to fertile farmlands and its attractiveness to skilled immigrants due to policies of religious and ethnic tolerance, also created a kind of urban magnetism. To become a major urban center a city also had to develop financial services fundamental to the conduct and growth of trade. The goodness of nature, the policies of the proprietor, and the canniness of the merchants provided Philadelphia with all of these features.

During the 1680s and 1690s Philadelphia rapidly established itself as the chief port of the Delaware River, serving as the commercial entrepôt for Pennsylvania, West New Jersey, and the three Lower Counties on the Delaware. The old Delaware River ports—New Castle, Chester, and Burlington—became commercial satellites of Philadelphia. But the city's economic success was on a smaller scale than that of Boston and New York, and its economy did not develop along the lines anticipated by the proprietor and his chief English backers. Great things were expected of the Free Society of Traders in Pennsylvania, a joint-stock company incorporated by Penn in 1682. The company expected well-to-do Quaker merchants would market the colony's exports and select its imports. Furthermore, the society intended to handle Pennsylvania's fur trade with the Indians, build a glass factory, dig lead and iron mines, fish for whales, and produce linen cloth and wine for export. Little profit was realized from these efforts, and by 1686 the Free Society, headed for bankruptcy, abandoned its trading operations. Today this abortive commercial experiment survives only in the name it bequeathed to a Philadelphia neighborhood, Society Hill.

When William Penn left his city for the last time, in 1701, the new charter that he conferred upon Philadelphia raised the "greene Country Towne" of some 2,500 inhabitants to the status of a city. A Swedish pastor, Andreas Sandell, described the village between the Schuylkill and the Delaware as "a very pretty town" of some 500 brick houses in 1702, and by 1725 Christopher Saur estimated that there were "at least eight hundred important merchants and shopkeepers" in this "handsomely built" town. But the city's economy collapsed in the early 1720s due to the disastrous effects of the bursting of the so-called South Sea Bubble. In his *Autobiography* Benjamin Franklin remembered the look of the town upon his arrival in October 1723: "Most of the houses in Walnut Street between Second and Front Streets," he recalled, had "Bills on their Doors, to be let; and many likewise in Chestnut Street, and other Streets; which made me then think the Inhabitants of the City were one after another deserting it." Philadelphia's recovery from this depression was in part a cause and in part a result of the growth of the colony's population. Penn's tolerant, officially pacifist colony had from the beginning been attractive to European pietist sectarians from Germany and elsewhere. As the backcountry was transformed from forest to farm, Philadelphia's artisans and traders found new economic opportunities. These opportunities inspired larger families and also acted as a magnet to Europe's restless people; the end of the 1720s saw the commencement of a human flood of immigrants. Philadelphia's merchants and artisans thrived as they provided for the needs of an ever-increasing tide of humanity. In the nineteenth century Philadelphia would give way to New York as the immigrants' chief port of entry, but in the eighteenth Philadelphia was the funnel through which Europeans by the thousands passed on their way to creating new lives in America.

The filling of the backcountry meant a great surge in Pennsylvania's agricultural production, with obvious repercussions for Philadelphia's shipping and mercantile interests. Wheat, flour, and bread were the staple Philadelphia exports, as well as lumber products and flaxseed. Philadelphia merchants faced the same basic problem as Boston and New York merchants: how to acquire the English goods they wanted when they had very little to sell on the English market. They copied Boston and New York by looking to the West Indies: they shipped out Pennsylvania's agricultural surplus—meat, grain, and especially flour—as well as forest products, chiefly barrel staves for the West Indian rum trade. For these cargoes they received bills of exchange or sugar, with which they purchased manufactured goods.

Philadelphia was also mineral rich, and was soon viewed by English iron masters as a dangerous rival. In the early eighteenth century, the system of mercantilism was beginning to take hold, a system in which the colonies were seen as part of a closed trade monopoly dominated by the mother country, England, contributing to her power and wealth. The colonies and the mother country were to comprise a completely self-sufficient unit—the colonies supplying the raw materials to be transferred by the mother country into finished goods to be sold back to the colonies. Each of the two elements—colonies and mother country—would thus have a protected market and each would prosper. Pushed by English manufacturers as they became prominent in the economy and in politics, mercantilism was defined in legislation that prevented the colonies from producing finished goods in competition with England. An iron act of 1750 prohibited the erection of any new mills in the colonies for slitting, rolling, or plating iron, or of any new furnaces for making steel. At the time there were about a hundred small furnaces and forges in the colonies, most in Pennsylvania, the first sign of industrialization in an otherwise agricultural-commercial economy.

As the counting house took precedence over the meeting-house, many Quakers not only lost their zeal, but Quakerism in Philadelphia was losing its numerical preeminence as well. The growth of commerce and population transformed the city from a Quaker community to a religiously and philosophically heterogeneous one. By the mid-1740s, helped by Scotch-Irish immigration and the emergence of a diversity of religious denominations and sects, the cultural atmosphere, at least among the town's burgeoning upper class, moved away not only from Quakerism but also from traditional Christianity and toward the secularism of the Enlightenment. Philadelphia's Quakers were not only torn between their duty to God and to the world, they also found themselves increasingly a minority in their own country; by mid-century they made up only one-sixth of the population.

In the early eighteenth century the number of non-English arrivals grew to phenomenal proportions. Germans came, fleeing the depredations of war along the Rhine, religious persecution, the exactions of petty princes, and the remorseless pressure of economic change. For the most part they came to Pennsylvania; those affiliated with religious groups tended to settle as communities on the outer fringes of English settlement, while the rest came singly or with their families. But they too eventually settled on the fringe of the English, creating a German pale that extended in a great arc around Philadelphia. The Scotch-Irish came too; the Scots who had settled in northern Ireland early in the seventeenth century were subjected to rack-renting by absentee landlords and were struck by periodic crop failures. In great waves they left Ulster for America, some settling in New England but most landing in Philadelphia, and they also tended to move to the outer fringes of settlement. These two groups came to dominate the Pennsylvania backcountry, and from there they flowed southward to settle in western Maryland and the Shenandoah Valley of Virginia, with some pressing southeast into the Carolina Piedmont and southwest to the headwaters of the Tennessee River.

In 1724 ten master builders formed the Carpenters' Company of the City and County of Philadelphia to better instruct themselves in architecture. Three years later one of the members,

James Porteus, became the principal builder of the city's most ambitiously Palladian structure of the colonial era, the imposing Christ Church. When the church was completed in 1744, the Palladian window of its east front was still exceptional in the architectural design of an American building; setting off the customary horizontal symmetries with opulent detail was a graceful balustrade decorated with wooden urns imported from London. The legislature, having previously met in private rooms, appropriated funds for a government building in 1729 and named a building committee that included Andrew Hamilton. Hamilton, the legislature's speaker and a talented amateur architect, designed the Pennsylvania State House, later Independence Hall. The State House's red brick was set off with stone quoins, keystones, belt courses, and panels, marking the designers' intention that the structure should be monumentally worthy of the important institutions it housed.

There were also more mundane changes in the city's physical aspect that served to differentiate it from a crossroads town. By mid-century most of the streets had been paved with cobblestones or paving blocks and had brick or flagstone sidewalks, often bordered with posts to protect pedestrians from vehicular traffic. To one English visitor of 1765, Lord Adam Gordon, Philadelphia was a "great and noble City," now probably fourth in size among the cities of the British Empire, behind only London, Edinburgh, and Dublin.

An improved network of transportation and communication during the century's middle years also meant a growth in trade. By mid-century the most frequently used highway in America was the great Philadelphia Wagon Road that led out from the city to Lancaster; over it moved settlers seeking lands to the west, and, coming and going, wagons and caravans of supplies and trade goods. While overland transportation vastly improved during these years, the Atlantic remained Philadelphia's principal avenue of trade. So rapid was the growth in commerce that more waterfront construction took place in Philadelphia than in any other American port. Boston had been the great shipbuilding center of the American colonies, but by 1750 this primacy was passing to Philadelphia, due to a huge demand and the great supply of ash and cedar in Pennsylvania and West New Jersey. Near the waterfront and often in the neighborhood of the shipyards, other industries, large and small, operated. Many of them, such as the blacksmith shops, foundries, and sail lofts, were essential for the shipbuilding industry; there were also tanneries, distilleries, breweries, carriage shops, fulling mills, and cooperages.

Rhythms of Life in Colonial New York:
Artisans and Mechanicks of All Sorts Are Drawn Thither

New York probably had the most aristocratic social structure of all the British American colonies. Landlords in alliance with Manhattan merchants dominated the political and social scene, and in their manor houses the New York aristocracy, using the English nobility as their model, reproduced a genteel society along the banks of the Hudson in which family pride, Anglicanism, and conservative principles were judiciously fused. Generations of intermarriage and family alliances created a tightly knit clique with an intense class loyalty. Since most of the aristocracy belonged to the Church of England, they hated "dissenters" not only because of Cromwell and the Civil War in England but also because the Calvinists in New England were fighting an American episcopate. As officials they disliked the Yankees' challenges of New York's land claims along its eastern border, and as landholders they feared the spread of "leveling" ideas by New England farmers who contested land titles and led anti-rent wars. As true monarchists they looked askance at the republican principles taking root in New England. And as a proud caste they resented the cultural arrogance of New Englanders such as John Adams, who claimed there was not a cultured man in New York.

Although aristocratic families provided most of the political and cultural leaders of colonial New York, they had to pay considerable attention to the wishes of people such as the wholesalers, retailers, and independent handicraftsmen in the city and the independent and tenant farmers in the country. Agriculture was the mainstay of the colonial economy, directly supporting eighty percent of the population, and providing much of the livelihood of urban merchants and their employees.

Apart from agriculture, commerce was the outstanding feature of New York's provincial economy. Businessmen were quick to see and exploit the advantages of New York's fine harbor, central location, and magnificent approaches. Moreover, the agricultural development of the Hudson Valley provided both supply and demand for traders. Cotton, spices, beef and pork, flax, hemp, potash, and forest products were shipped to Britain, and boards, staves, and shingles were carried to the West Indies. New York's imports covered the whole range of manufactured goods, as well as some raw materials: clothing, furniture, hardware, tea, spices, gunpowder, paints, drugs, and coal, among other products. Luxury items also became important imports as the aristocracy gained affluence. Although mercantilism permeated the thinking of British statesmen and provincial officials throughout the colonial period, the restrictive framework of imperial, provincial, and municipal regulations and duties were often evaded through undercover trade or smuggling.

Manufacturing developed slowly in New York because of the scarcity of skilled labor, the lack of banking facilities, mercantile regulations imposed by Britain, and the availability of cheap English goods. The manufacturing that did exist was closely associated with the processing of foodstuffs and lumber: sawmills and gristmills accompanied the northward and westward push of settlers, and breweries and distilleries used up local grain products and furnished easily transported products. For the most part, local craftsmen supplied the needs of the rapidly expanding settlement on the Hudson River.

American colonists were unable to increase their purchases of European goods during the eighteenth century in proportion to the needs of a population that doubled every twenty-five years. With each decade the differential became greater and was made up by manufacturing in the colonies. Crafts took hold in emerging towns and villages, and artisans began to specialize, certain of demand for their wares. Given ample resources, a maturing economy, and an expanding market, the minds of urban craftsmen turned to ways of increasing production and to invention. In 1772, on the eve of the American Revolution, General Thomas Gage effectively summed up the colonial manufacturer situation in a letter to Lord Barrington: "I [think it would] be for our interest to Keep the Settlers within reach of the Sea-Coast as long as we can; and to cramp their Trade as far as it can be done prudentially. Cities flourish and increase by extensive Trade, Artisans and Mechanicks

of all sorts are drawn thither, who Teach all sorts of Handicraft work before unknown in the Country, and they soon come to make for themselves what they used to import."

The most important element in the development of craftwork was the growth and concentration of the population. Many Old World artisans, impressed by stories of high wages, good markets, better prices, and freedom from medieval guild restrictions, ventured across the ocean to try their fortune in America. Huguenot, Scotch-Irish, and German craftsmen arrived in nearly every ship after 1720, but it was Englishmen who made the greatest contribution to the handicrafts of America's earliest cities. Although it was the great age of British craftsmanship and enterprise, to many journeymen the land seemed brighter to the west, and they sailed away from London, Bristol, Manchester, and Hull. Regular arrivals of skilled artisans ensured the transit of modes, styles, inventions, and techniques to America almost as soon as they developed abroad, and the increased competition incited colonial craftsmen to improve their workmanship. In the largest coastal cities, and later in other rising towns, immigrants taught native Americans their techniques and methods, and new skills and new crafts were steadily introduced along with new ideas, so that when independence came the country was ready to embark on its own course of manufacturing. Tench Coxe acknowledged the debt in 1794 in his *View of the United States of America:* "A large proportion of the most successful manufacturers in the United States consists of persons, who were journeymen, and in a few instances were foremen in the work-shops and manufactories of Europe; who as having been skillful, sober, frugal, and having thus saved a little money, have set up for themselves with great advantage in America."

The split between England and America grew ever wider during the 1760s and early 1770s. The focal point for discontent was in the realm of economics, but this uneasiness was generated in the social, cultural, and political spheres of living as well. During the 1760s, a broad coalition of Americans resisted new tax levies and attempts by the British to tighten controls over the provincial governments. Once linked unquestioningly to Great Britain, politically and culturally aware colonists had begun to develop a sense of their own identity as Americans.

Quaker Philadelphia:

Stability and Crisis, Population Growth and Ethnic Diversity

Philadelphia was the commercial, intellectual, and cultural capital of the colonies. Even its physical surroundings impressed visitors as eminently suitable for pleasurable living. Philadelphia, wrote one foreign observer in the middle of the eighteenth century, needed only the streets to be paved "to make it appear to advantage, for there is few towns if any in England that are better Illumin'd with Lamps, & those of the best Sort, nor their watch better regulated." As the largest city in America, Philadelphia was a natural site for the First Continental Congress, which met in Philadelphia in the new and still incomplete Carpenters' Hall in September 1774. While the city proper still adhered to Penn's plan of eight east-west streets, its constantly increasing population spilled into the "liberties"—German artisans clustering in the northern tier and tenant farmers attracted to the Southwark section. Its population, estimated between 23,700 and 35,000, ranked in the top seven cities of the British empire, most likely about fourth. There were an estimated 5,340 buildings, principally brick, concentrated in the narrow corridor between Front and Fourth streets, and some sixteen churches, including meetinghouses and synagogues, catering to the spiritually minded, while several hundred stores, lined almost solidly the length of Second Street, and along Market to Third, offered a wide variety of items, both imported and domestic.

With the growth of wealth and the secularization of colonial life, American achievement in the arts and crafts reached a high order that revealed the impress of the English parent pattern. Although utilitarian standards always conditioned colonial manufacturing and crafts, there were individuals whose aesthetic sense was never so dulled as to be unappreciative of beauty in its diverse manifestations. Colonial artists, when corresponding with Europeans, were inclined to say, a little defiantly and a little apologetically, that they were self-taught. But in Philadelphia the brilliant Chippendale style in mahogany furniture demonstrated the brilliance of colonial achievement and was seen in all its glory ornamenting the city's principal mansions. Architecture in Philadelphia also came into its own in the 1760s and 1770s, with the erection of many fine urban mansions. Builders such as David Evans and Robert Smith built houses whose interiors displayed splendid paneling, carving, and gilding, impressive chimney pieces, elaborate stucco ceilings, portraits by Charles Willson Peale, silver by Philip Syng and the Richardsons, and furniture from the shops of Benjamin Randolph, Thomas Affleck, James Reynolds, and William Savery, among others.

In June 1744, Dr. Alexander Hamilton, a canny Scottish-born physician living in Annapolis, paid his first visit to the Quaker town of Philadelphia. Hamilton was an astute observer of mid-eighteenth-century Philadelphia, and there he encountered two quite different worlds. One consisted of men of his own status, the merchants and professionals Hamilton mingled with at the Governor's Club, which he called "the better sort . . . a society of gentlemen that met at a tavern every night and converse on various subjects." He reacted differently to the other world of Philadelphia, that composed of people he variously termed "rabble," "a strange medley," or "comicall, grotesque phuizzes," most of whom spoke, he thought, "ignorantly" regardless of the subject. The residents' chief employment, he wrote, "is traffick and mercantile business"; and the richest merchants of all were the Quakers. Members of that sect also controlled the government of Pennsylvania, but, Hamilton noted, "the standing or falling of the Quakers in the House of Assembly depends upon their making sure the interest of the [German] Palatines in this province, who of late have turned so numerous that they can sway the votes which way they please."

Hamilton correctly recognized that the Quakers maintained control of Pennsylvania politics because they had managed to win the support of recent German immigrants. In addition, Hamilton accurately assessed the importance of commerce in Americans' lives. The web of imperial trade woven before 1720 became even more complex and all-encompassing during the next fifty years.

In 1763 the British Ministry, at the urging of George Grenville, chancellor of the exchequer, projected a defense plan for North America which required the recruitment and maintenance of an army of 10,000 men. To the British, a people already heavily taxed, it seemed reasonable to shift part of the cost to the colonists, the direct beneficiaries of the protective force. Parliament responded with measures that seriously and directly affected all colonial entrepreneurs. The three pieces of legislation that produced the most violent reactions in Philadelphia were the Stamp Act of 1765, the Townshend Revenue Acts of 1767, and modifications of the Tea Act in 1773. American opposition to the new British tax measures was fairly predictable. The response in Philadelphia showed an intensity of feeling, expressed by people of all classes, that could only emanate from a community conscious of having suffered deep and serious injury. Proof of this was found in the ease with which chiming bells and pounding drums could summon crowds of 8,000 people to the State House yard to act on the latest developments. It found expression in the newspapers, then becoming more aware of the influence they wielded in forming public opinion. It burst forth passionately in the taverns and howled through the streets with the mobs. It put in ferment a city whose government was complacent and content, and generated mass meetings as vehicles of expression and committees as agents of force in a community that came to accept them almost as a way of life.

Philadelphia's merchants were goaded into nonimportation agreements by threats of mob violence by mechanics and artisans and members of the lower orders, and impelled into action by the influence of the Philadelphia press. Radical in their opposition to the unpopular British measures, Philadelphia's newspapers not only reported but stimulated events. The *Pennsylvania Chronicle*, beginning in the early winter of 1767, published a series of letters that exceeded in their influence and circulation almost any other publication of the Revolutionary era. These, the famous "Farmer's Letters" of John Dickinson, were copied in colonial newspapers everywhere and later published in pamphlet form as *Letters from a Farmer in Pennsylvania to the Inhabitants of the British Colonies*. The "farmer" was actually an outstanding Philadelphia lawyer who in trenchant and logical prose advocated caution and nonviolent action, constructed a brief for constitutional government, and maintained that the colonies needed to unite their efforts, for the cause of one was "the cause of all." Dickinson may well be regarded as the first "Continental" spokesman, the first prenational patriotic hero; next to Franklin, he was possibly the best known Philadelphian of the pre-Revolutionary era.

The Philadelphia which became the nation's temporary capital in 1790 stretched about nine blocks north and south along the Delaware River and not far beyond the State House to the west. The population of the city and the adjacent districts,

estimated at 38,798 in 1782, grew to 42,520 by the first federal census of 1790, despite the effects of war. Refurbishing since the war had made much of the city attractive again, with red-brick houses facing red-brick foot pavements, rows of buttonwood, willow, and Lombardy poplar trees, main streets paved with pebbles and with brick or wooden gutters, and posts between carriage ways and footpaths to protect pedestrians. A Philadelphia County courthouse was erected along Chestnut Street just west of the State House in 1787–89, and to balance it a city hall rose to the east of the State House in 1790–91; these buildings followed traditional Philadelphia red-brick Georgian lines, though cupolas gave them a slight air of pretension. With the arrival of the federal government, the courthouse became Congress Hall, accommodating the House of Representatives on its first floor and the Senate on the second; City Hall took in the United States Supreme Court. The new library building the Library Company built in 1789–90 signaled the beginning of architectural change in the city; designed by William Thornton, a young physician recently arrived from the West Indies, Library Hall had an elegance and delicacy of detail hitherto rarely seen in Philadelphia, with its four pilasters and ornamental balustrade.

On December 14, 1799, George Washington died at Mount Vernon. The legislature adjourned when confirmation of the death arrived, and the mayor requested that the bells of Christ Church be muffled for three days "as a mark of deep regret with which the citizens of this place view the melancholy news." Congressional chambers, churches, and particularly the pew that Washington had occupied at Christ Church were shrouded in black. Representative Henry Lee of Virginia, who he had known Washington long and well, was chosen by Congress to deliver the oration. "First in war, first in peace, and first in the hearts of his countrymen," Lee said of Washington. "Such was the man for whom our nation mourns." With Washington gone and the capital about to move, the Federal era's greatness was passing. In the new century Philadelphia's position as the leading American city would soon be lost. New York soon became the largest and richest American city, and after the federal capital moved to Washington, Philadelphia also lost its political preeminence. In 1799 rural suspicion of the city and a desire for a more central location shifted the state government to Lancaster; it moved again to Harrisburg in 1812.

Van Cortlandt Manor in Croton-on-Hudson, New York, built in the late seventeenth century and remodeled in 1749 by Pierre Van Cortlandt I, is furnished largely with objects that belonged to the Van Cortlandt family and were used during their 250-year occupancy, which stretched from the late seventeenth century through the early years of the twentieth century. The manor house and outbuildings were the center of a vast estate devoted to farming, milling, and trade. The Van Cortlandts were patriots during the Revolution, and this accounts for the survival of the family furnishings. While most large landholders wanted a national government strong enough to protect property rights and therefore endorsed the Federalist position, Pierre Van Cortlandt was one of the few who were numbered among the Anti-Federalists.

opposite page

In the parlor in Philipsburg Manor, Upper Mills, North Tarrytown, New York, the center table has been laid with a linen cloth laden with fruit, tarts, cake, glazed fruit, and cinnamon sticks—all traditional to the Dutch-English Christmas celebration. Many of the early Hudson River valley settlers were Dutch Protestants and Huguenots who brought with them the manners and customs of the European lowlands. After the English seized New Netherland in 1664, the colony was infused with new traditions. Many of the Dutch and Huguenots converted to the Anglican church, although Dutch as a language persisted in certain areas well into the nineteenth century and the text of prayer books was often printed in both English and Dutch.

The portrait of two children over the mantel in the living room of the collection of Helaine and Burton Fendelman, Westchester County, New York, is attributed to Zedekiah Belknap, and the New Hampshire fireboard is attributed to Rufus Porter. The grain-painted, six-board blanket chest in the foreground was made in New England in the early nineteenth century, as was the document box on top of it, which is decorated with an eagle and the initials "A B."

View of the Abraham Hasbrouck house in New Paltz, New York,
with the Dutch Reformed Church, built in 1839 and enlarged in
1872, in the background at left. Persecution had driven Huguenot
families from Europe; once here, they settled in the neighboring
towns of Kingston (then known as Wiltwyck) and Hurley before
banding together to found New Paltz, named in memory of the
Rheinland Pfalz. As the town prospered in the late seventeenth
century, the founding fathers began replacing their original log
dwellings with sturdy one-room stone houses. These new houses
had thick native-stone walls held together by clay-and-straw mortar,
enormous beams attached to the walls with iron bolts, and wide,
thick floorboards of pine or hemlock. Pine shingles covered the
roofs, and squat wooden gutters drained into rain barrels that
provided water for household use. Basements were built to store
perishable food, and attics for storing grain. Almost all the stone
houses in New Paltz have a low rectangular outline set off by
a single-slant roof.

140

The earliest section of the Abraham Hasbrouck house was completed by 1693, and by 1712 two additions were in place. New Paltz was settled in 1678 by Huguenots who, the year before, had been granted a patent for a parcel of land lying in the Wallkill River valley between the Shawangunk Mountains and the Hudson River. Besides obtaining the patent from the English governor of New York, the twelve founding fathers, also known as the "patentees," paid the Esopus Indians for the land. It was probably this attention to the Indians' rights, ignored by the settlers of nearby towns, that made it possible for the Huguenots to live in peace with the original inhabitants.

The mantelpiece in the south parlor of the Mulford-Baker House, East Hampton, New York, is surmounted by a portrait of an unidentified boy, New England, of about 1835. It is a comparatively rare example of the pastel medium, which never became as popular here as it was in Europe. Young children wore coral beads for luck, and boys wore dresses with pantaloons, as seen here, until the age of six or so, when they were considered old enough for trousers. The excellent proportions and relative simplicity of the woodwork reflect the refinement of a prosperous but conservative town such as East Hampton at the turn of the nineteenth century. The American spongeware jugs on the mantel date from the late nineteenth and early twentieth centuries.

opposite page
A portrait of Captain William Martin of Warren, Rhode Island, painted by Joseph Whiting Stock, in the west parlor of the Mulford-Baker House, East Hampton, New York, hangs above a late-eighteenth-century slant-front desk from eastern New England. In front of the desk is a Massachusetts Queen Anne side chair, made about 1750–80. In the left foreground, a pair of Connecticut River valley cherry chairs of about 1770 flank a New Hampshire tea table, made about 1740–70.

A portrait of Mrs. William Martin and her daughter Julia, painted by Joseph Whiting Stock, hangs in the west parlor of the Mulford-Baker House. On the Massachusetts mahogany card table of about 1800 is English creamware of about the same date.

opposite page
The dining table in the Mulford-Baker House is set with English creamware plates, candlesticks, and a reticulated basket, all 1790–1820; English salt-glazed pottery sauceboats, 1760–80; and English and Continental late-eighteenth-century wineglasses and champagne flutes. The cherry dining room chairs, from a set of six, are from the Connecticut River valley, made about 1800. Beneath the portrait of Adaline F. Pierce, painted by Alexander C. McClean in Boston in 1835, is an Irish marble-topped carved mahogany table of about 1750, on which is a collection of late-eighteenth-century English and Irish decanters. Above the mantel hangs an early-eighteenth-century English looking glass, and on the mantel shelf are French porcelain urns and painted American fire shields.

In the east bedroom of the Mulford-Baker House, the late-eighteenth-century New England maple pencil-post bed is dressed for summer with nineteenth-century English cottons. Flanking the fireplace are two chairs made at the Shaker community in Mount Lebanon, New York, in the early twentieth century. The brass warming pan dates from the early nineteenth century. Above the mantel hangs a New England theorem painting of about 1835.

opposite page

The corner cupboard in the dining room of the Mulford-Baker House contains mid-eighteenth-century English salt-glazed stoneware. The cherry shield-back dining room chairs are from the Connecticut River valley, made about 1800.

An early-nineteenth-century New England painted corner
cupboard in the south parlor of the Mulford-Baker House contains
part of a large collection of American spongeware, a utilitarian
stoneware with decoration based on English painted ceramics.
Spongeware was first produced in New Jersey, Pennsylvania, and
Ohio in the mid-nineteenth century, and remained popular well
into the twentieth.

View across the Hudson River from Clermont, Germantown, New York, built by Robert Livingston Jr. between 1730 and 1750 and rebuilt between 1779 and 1782. Visible across the river are the peaks of the Catskill Mountains that inspired the estate's name: Clermont means "clear mountain" in French. Seven successive generations of the politically and socially prominent Livingston family of New York left their imprint on the architecture, room interiors, and landscape at Clermont. The estate was established in 1728 when Robert Livingston Jr. inherited a tract of 13,000 acres along the Hudson River from his father, Robert Sr., first Lord of Livingston Manor. The manor comprised the southern third of modern Columbia County and was the second-largest private landholding in colonial New York. Robert of Clermont's only child, Judge Robert R. Livingston, added to the family's landholdings when he married Margaret Beekman, heir to immense tracts of land in Dutchess and Ulster counties, in the 1740s. Their eldest son, Chancellor Robert R. Livingston, entered into a partnership with the inventor Robert Fulton, and their steamboat, the *Clermont*, embarked on its maiden voyage between New York City and Albany in 1807, setting off the transportation revolution in the United States.

The Morris-Jumel Mansion in Washington Heights, New York City, was built in 1765 by Roger Morris, a lieutenant colonel in the British army. The Palladian villa, with its double-height portico, colossal columns, and triangular pediment, may have been designed by Morris himself, whose father was a noted eighteenth-century British architect. As British troops withdrew from their occupation of Manhattan in the fall of 1776, the house was used briefly by General Washington as his headquarters; on July 10, 1790, President Washington returned to the house for a nostalgic dinner with several members of his cabinet. In 1810 the house was bought by Stephen Jumel, a wealthy French emigrant merchant and shipowner, who lived there with his wife, Eliza Bowen. The nineteenth-century four-post bed in this bedroom, once owned by Eliza, was probably made in New York. The cotton bedspread was made by Phoebe Philips Eddy in the late eighteenth century, and the mahogany bedsteps date from the nineteenth century.

Eliza Bowen, the wife of Stephen Jumel, who purchased the Morris-Jumel Mansion in 1810, was an unusual woman. Beautiful and brilliant, the daughter of an impoverished family from Providence, Rhode Island, she had been Jumel's mistress and was said to have worked as a prostitute. New York society rejected her, but, unfazed, the Jumels lavishly redecorated and refurbished the house in high French Empire style, importing many objects from Paris, including a bed reputed to have belonged to Napoleon. After her husband died in 1832, Eliza (who was widely regarded as one of the wealthiest women in New York) married the disgraced former vice president of the United States, Aaron Burr—a liaison that failed after six months. She lived on in the mansion and became steadily more eccentric; she sometimes traveled in Europe calling herself "Madame Burr, ex vice-Queen of America."

Ephrata Cloister, near Lancaster, Pennsylvania, was a religious commune founded in 1732 by Conrad Beissel, a mystic who had come to Germantown, Pennsylvania, from his native Germany twelve years before. The Almonry, possibly built about 1733 (left), Saal ("Hall" in German), built 1741 (center), and Sisters' House, built 1743 (right), are the most architecturally significant buildings at the Cloister. The stone Almonry is built into a hillside; the ground floor was the community bakery, while the second floor served as a hostel which provided free food and lodging for male travelers.

The Saal contains rooms for worship, living, and storage. Ephrata, the Hebrew word for plentiful, was an early name for Bethlehem. Ephrata Cloister members lived a monastic life of work and religious devotion, according to the tenets of German pietists who had influenced Beissel when he was a young man. The emphasis in the Cloister was on mystical revelation and brotherhood rather than on ritual and creed. The faithful celebrated the Sabbath on Saturday, as Jews do, and on occasion they observed communion and the early-Christian practice of washing the feet as a symbolic act of humility.

The five-story Saal at Ephrata Cloister, Ephrata, Pennsylvania, built in 1741, contains the meeting room where the congregation gathered for Sabbath worship every Saturday. Ephrata was neither the first nor the largest utopian community in antebellum America, but it was among the most durable of the pietistic groups. By the middle of the eighteenth century its numbers may have reached three hundred; in 1900 there were seventeen remaining brethren and sisters. Ephratans, and most pietists, never intended to proselytize. Spiritual contemplation was the essence of Ephrata; for the faithful, heaven on earth was not a distant hope but an immediate expectation. These earnest utopians had great confidence in their way of life. Detaching themselves from worldly society, freed of its imperfections, they believed they would create an ideal social system made up of truly moral men and women.

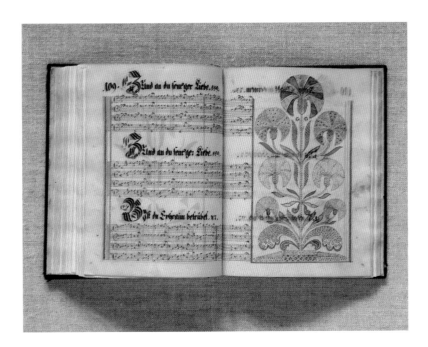

The designs on these pages from a manuscript hymnal produced at
Ephrata Cloister about 1750 represent the flowering of the spiritual
life as expressed through the hymns, many of which were composed
at the Cloister. The texts to the hymns are from the *Weyrauchs-Hugel*,
a hymnbook printed for the Cloister in 1739 by Christopher Sauer
of Germantown, Pennsylvania.

Each of the three floors of the Sisters' House at Ephrata Cloister had a separate kitchen, where food for the sisters living on that floor was prepared. The stone sink between the windows has a drain that leads through the log wall to the outside. The eighteenth-century poplar table was made at the Cloister and stands on a copy of the original lime-mortar floor. The Ephrata Society consisted of three orders: a celibate sisterhood, a celibate brotherhood, and a married order of householders. Dressed in long white hooded habits, the celibates toiled twelve hours a day farming and growing fruit on the society's two hundred acres. They also ran grist, paper, saw, fulling, and oil mills and a print shop and bindery. The sisters were responsible for baking, making cloth, and cooking the one meager vegetarian meal that the celibates were allowed each day.

These buildings at Ephrata Cloister now house the printing and binding operations at the cloister. The building at left, built about 1732, may be the oldest surviving building on the site. The adjoining house dates from the early nineteenth century. Printing was an important occupation at the cloister from 1743 until 1793, but the original print shop no longer survives. The cloister faithful constructed their buildings in the styles of their native Rhineland. Mostly built between 1735 and 1750, they have been restored to their original appearance and furnished to illustrate the way of life of their original occupants.

This breezeway at the Peter Wentz Farmstead in Worcester, Pennsylvania, connects the summer and winter kitchens. Cooking took place in the summer kitchen during the hot months, and baking and such dirty jobs as butchering and soap- and candle-making were done there all year long.

The Pennsylvania walnut Pembroke table of about 1750 stands between Philadelphia walnut arm and side chairs, made around 1760, in the parlor of the Peter Wentz Farmstead. On the table are pieces from a *famille rose* china trade tea set and a silver cream jug made in London, datemarked 1774/5. In the fireplace is a pair of brass-and-iron andirons made in Philadelphia about 1740; the brazier in front of the fireplace would have been filled with hot coals and taken to a spot in the room that required additional heat. On the window seat, an urban architectural feature seldom found in rural houses, is a cherry tape loom, which was used by the women and children of the family to produce fabric less than one inch wide.

163

The late-eighteenth-century two-drawer pine blanket chest in this unheated, sparsely furnished upstairs bedroom in the Peter Wentz Farmstead was made in Pennsylvania. On it is a chintz quilt of the same period. Hanging on the peg rail above are a pair of linen breeches, a cotton-print petticoat, and a wooden wrench used to tighten the ropes that supported the mattresses on the beds. The masonry shelf is built into the chimney pile of the winter-kitchen fireplace and served as a warming shelf for blankets.

The main bedroom in the Peter Wentz Farmstead is dominated by a country high-post maple bed painted red and made about 1760. On it are homespun linens and a late-eighteenth-century chintz quilt; the cradle of about 1765, originally painted blue and salmon, is also made up with homespun linens and a chintz crib quilt. The pine two-drawer blanket chest was made locally around 1770 and retains an old, but not its original, coat of green paint.

The Farmstead's furnishings, based on Wentz's inventory of 1794, reflect both the proximity of the house to Philadelphia and Wentz's station in life. Good but not elaborate pieces of Philadelphia and English furniture are displayed with objects believed to be of local manufacture. The total absence of window hangings, carpets, and the like is substantiated by Wentz's inventory and contemporary inventories of individuals of similar standing.

The pent eave between the first and second stories of Wright's Ferry Mansion, Columbia, Pennsylvania, is characteristic of the early Georgian style as interpreted by English Quakers in Pennsylvania. The red oak shingles, side-lapped against the prevailing wind and with the butts nailed, are indicative of the local German workmen who undoubtedly helped construct the house. Opening up southeastern Pennsylvania was important for secure westward expansion. In 1730, with James Logan's assistance, the Wrights obtained patents for a ferry service across the Susquehanna River and for a road from the ferry to the town of Lancaster, the seat of Lancaster County, which had been set off from Chester County in 1729. As the Wrights had been instrumental in establishing the new county, it was named in honor of their native Lancashire.

The early-Georgian character of the parlor of Wright's Ferry Mansion is apparent in the architectural paneling, though the arched doors with their keystones are somewhat less sophisticated than those in Philadelphia houses. The maple daybed with a rush seat was made in eastern Pennsylvania about 1740; such "couch chairs," as they were called in inventories, were a luxury found only in affluent households. The brilliance of design and control of line so exquisitely exercised by Philadelphia cabinetmakers during the Queen Anne period are evident in the walnut easy chair, made in that city about 1740. In keeping with the austerity of the interior, wool rather than silk damask has been used on this chair and throughout the house. Both the English Quaker heritage of the house's original owner and her ties to Philadelphia are strongly evident in the house's architecture and furnishings.

opposite page
The staircase beside the kitchen fireplace at Wright's Ferry Mansion leads to the servants' rooms. The restoration and furnishing of the building reflects the elegance and simplicity of design typical of Quaker households. Following surviving inventories of Quaker homes from the same region and period, the floors and windows have been left bare and the rooms sparsely furnished.

168

There are many closets in Wright's Ferry Mansion, more than are generally found in early-eighteenth-century dwellings. The paneling throughout the house is tulip poplar; here, in the principal bedroom, it has simply been waxed. The eastern Pennsylvania commode chair, made about 1750, with a pewter chamber pot, is one of the finest ladderback commode chairs known. The rare wrought-iron candlestand was made in eastern Pennsylvania in the first half of the eighteenth century and has the bold scrolling frequently encountered in Philadelphia ironwork of the period. Although Philadelphia would have been Susanna Wright's primary source for furnishings, she also patronized local Germanic sources for utilitarian items.

171

View of the staircase in the entry hall of Wright's Ferry Mansion, built in 1738 for Susanna Wright. In 1726, about the time that James Logan was making plans to build his country mansion, Stenton, in Germantown, Susanna Wright and her father, John, purchased a hundred acres in western Chester County, an isolated spot on the east bank of the Susquehanna River. Wright and her family were among several prominent English Quakers from Chester and Darby, Pennsylvania, to settle at this remote crossing on the Susquehanna River, ten miles west of Lancaster. To make up for the want of city company and conversation, Susanna Wright maintained a lively correspondence with friends in Philadelphia, who included many of the best minds of the colonies.

The two-story, one-bay-deep section to the right of the back door of the house at John Bartram's Garden in Philadelphia, Pennsylvania, comprises the original Swedish farmhouse, which had a gambrel roof. When Bartram built the east facade in 1770, he extended the other side of the house by the depth of one room. The one-story addition at the left and a corresponding one at the opposite end of the building were added in the 1820s by Ann Bartram Carr, his granddaughter, who installed the dormers at the same time.

opposite page

View from the hall of the original Swedish house at John Bartram's Garden into the kitchen added by Bartram in 1731. A protégé of James Logan, John Bartram was a self-educated artisan-scientist and the first American botanist. When he was introduced to Peter Collinson, a leading light in the Royal Society and the center of the transatlantic natural history circle, he said of Bartram that he was a "down right plain Country Man" and a "Quaker too Into the Bargain." Primarily a noble nurseryman, seedsman, and farmer, Bartram traveled throughout the American colonies, much like an itinerant Quaker minister, collecting botanical specimens rather than converting souls.

The parlor of the Bartram house, Philadelphia, Pennsylvania, and the adjoining hall comprised the ground floor of the original Swedish house. The cherry slant-front desk and mahogany looking glass and side chairs are all American eighteenth-century pieces. The American lusterware teacups and saucers on the table date from about 1830 and originally belonged to Elizabeth Bartram Wright, a granddaughter of the botanist. Bartram left the part of his estate that included the house and botanical garden to his son John Jr., who shared his father's interest in horticulture. Another of Bartram's sons, William, lived with his brother and his family following a four-year botanical expedition to the Deep South. William and John changed the botanical garden into a successful commercial nursery called John Bartram and Son. They put out their first catalog in 1783, offering plants and seeds for sale.

View of the kitchen at John Bartram's Garden, Philadelphia,
Pennsylvania, added by Bartram in 1731, and beyond it, the pantry.

This second-floor hall is part of the original, late-seventeenth-century house built by Swedish farmers at John Bartram's Garden. Bartram's first wife, Mary Maris, bore him two sons before she died in 1727. In 1729 he married Ann Mendenhall, also a Quaker, who bore him nine children; one child died young from each of the two marriages, so a total of nine children grew up in this small house. By 1731 Bartram added a kitchen with a bedroom above it. Then, in 1770, largely with his own hands, he extended the river facade of the house by the depth of one room, faced it with local stone, and changed the gambrel to a peaked roof.

The Hans Herr House in Lancaster, Pennsylvania, built in 1719 by Christian Herr, served as a residence for Christian and Anna Herr and his aging parents and as a meetinghouse for the Mennonite community's Sunday worship. The sandy limestone that forms the thick walls was quarried on the property; the oak forest surrounding the farmstead provided wood for the roof and interior partitions. This was one of the first stone houses in the settlement, and replaced the Herrs' earlier log house. In size and style, it is comparable to the medieval farmhouses the Mennonites had known in the Old World. When the house was finished, Christian Herr carved his initials and the year 1719 into the stone lintel over the front door. Similar houses were built by other German immigrants, but the Hans Herr House is one of the few remaining buildings of its kind in North America.

This sandstone building served as General George Washington's headquarters in 1777–78 at Valley Forge, Pennsylvania. It was built in 1768–70 and sublet to Washington by Deborah Hewes, who had rented the home from the original owner, Isaac Potts. A log addition was placed behind the building after it became clear that the house could not accommodate the commander in chief and his staff. After the failures at Brandywine and Germantown in December 1777, Washington took his army into winter quarters at Valley Forge, twenty miles northwest of Philadelphia. The strategic location placed his army between the occupied city of Philadelphia and the Continental Congress (forced to move to York), and helped protect the food supply that western Pennsylvania provided. In the dreadful winter of 1777–78, Washington reported from Valley Forge that 4,000 of his men were "unfit for duty because they were bare foot and otherwise naked." That winter's suffering has made Valley Forge a synonym for sacrifice in American wars. The American army survived its ordeal and, indeed, emerged from it a more efficient force.

Joseph Nicholson purchased this property in 1733 and built the front section of the building, now the White Swan Tavern in Chestertown, Maryland, about 1733–50. In 1793 his widow, Mary Hopper Nicholson, sold the property to John Bordley, who held the property until 1801.

While the use of the building in the eighteenth century is unknown, nineteenth-century newspaper advertisements document its use as a tavern and inn. When the building was listed for sale in 1853 in the *Kent News*, it was "considered the best tavern stand in town."

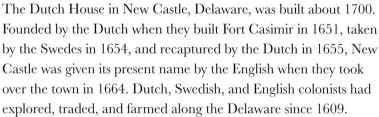

The Dutch House in New Castle, Delaware, was built about 1700. Founded by the Dutch when they built Fort Casimir in 1651, taken by the Swedes in 1654, and recaptured by the Dutch in 1655, New Castle was given its present name by the English when they took over the town in 1664. Dutch, Swedish, and English colonists had explored, traded, and farmed along the Delaware since 1609.

View of the Presbyterian Church in New Castle, Delaware, built about 1707. The landing place of William Penn in 1682, New Castle was the colonial capital of the Lower Counties "upon Delaware" until 1776. Helped by Scotch-Irish immigration, Presbyterians grew to rival the powerful Quakers in numbers in colonial Pennsylvania and Delaware.

Mount Cuba, outside Wilmington, Delaware, was designed by
Victorine and Samuel Homsey for Pamela Cunningham and
Lammot du Pont Copeland, and built in 1936–37. Its design is
derived from eighteenth-century plantation houses in James River,
Virginia, and its interior is fitted with finely crafted Southern
woodwork taken from now-demolished colonial homes.

The mahogany desk-and-bookcase in the living room at Mount
Cuba was made for the Potts family of Pottstown, Pennsylvania.
The Philadelphia craftsmen Thomas Affleck and James Reynolds
probably executed this masterpiece. The central finial of the desk-
and-bookcase is a brilliantly realized bust of the philosopher
John Locke, one of fewer than a dozen portrait busts known on
Philadelphia case furniture. The upholstered Philadelphia side
chair of about 1770 in front of the desk-and-bookcase is similar
to the set at Benjamin Chew's home, Cliveden, in Germantown,
Pennsylvania. The easy chair was made in Philadelphia, 1760–70.
Between the windows hangs what may be a portrait of Philadelphia
mariner John Gano, thought to be by the artist Charles Willson
Peale. The carpet is a Feraghan.

184

Dominating the dining room at Mount Cuba is a magnificent Philadelphia mahogany chest on chest of about 1765. Its cartouche, finials, and pediment carving retain their original gilded highlights. On pedestals flanking it are early-nineteenth-century German silver-gilt compotes. The Massachusetts mahogany marble-topped table at left, about 1755–60, is one of two set in classical symmetry against the piers of the window wall. On it is an early-nineteenth-century Sheffield tea urn. Lilies and daisies decorate the late-eighteenth-century English mahogany triple-pedestal dining table, around which is an assembled set of Philadelphia mahogany chairs of about 1770–90. The paneling is from a house of 1750–75 in Stafford County, Virginia.

The so-called Chinese hall at Mount Cuba is hung with late-eighteenth-century Chinese paper, in the manner of the Chinese Parlor at the Winterthur Museum. The camelback sofa and Chippendale side chair with a trefoil splat in the manner of James Gillingham are both Philadelphia mahogany pieces of about 1770. In the middle ground, flanked by broad, arched openings, is the vaulted cross hall; beyond are the paneled walls of the entrance hall. In this complex architectural enfilade, the rich textural assemblage of ornamental wallpapers, Oriental carpets, paneled walls, and antique American furniture comes to life in the soft incandescence of sconces and chandeliers.

The stately paneled walls of the principal bedroom of Mount
Cuba, crowned with a full Doric entablature, were taken from a
house of 1750–75 in King and Queen County, Virginia, where they
must have formed the main parlor. The furniture is mostly from
Philadelphia, and most was originally intended for a bedroom,
particularly the scroll-topped mahogany high chest of drawers of
about 1755–65 and the blue upholstered easy chair of about
1755–75. The splendid Philadelphia mahogany bedstead dates
from 1790–1800.

190

The paneling in the guest bedroom at Mount Cuba came from the Old Brick House in Pasquotank County, North Carolina, built about 1750–75. The walnut desk on frame with scalloped skirt and trifid feet in the manner of William Savery is from Pennsylvania, about 1745–55. Pulled up to it is a Philadelphia mahogany side chair of about 1770–80. The cherry couch, or daybed, made in Connecticut about 1770, is one of only three known examples with a Gothic splat, gadrooned skirt, and straight legs with crossed stretchers.

English mezzotints of the continents, published by John Fairburn in 1798, hang on the wall of the stairway of Poplar Hall, near Dover, Delaware. The face of the mahogany tall-case clock on the landing is inscribed "Duncan/Beard/Appoquinimink." Beard, a clockmaker, silversmith, and gunsmith, worked near Appoquinimink (now Odessa), Delaware, from 1767 until his death in 1797.

opposite page

Poplar Hall, near Dover, Delaware, was begun before 1740 by John Dickinson's father on the banks of the Saint Jones River. The house sits at the center of a plantation covering six square miles of Kent County. The main section was rebuilt by Dickinson after a fire in 1804; the five-bay facade of the house is characteristic of large Delaware farmhouses. The adjoining wing was added in the 1790s and contains the dining room, with a separate entrance and a bedroom above. Here John Dickinson grew up and was tutored at home before going to Philadelphia in 1750 to read law under John Moland, the king's attorney. In 1753 he sailed for England to study at the Inns of Court, carrying with him letters of introduction to Thomas Penn, the proprietor of the colony. When he returned to Philadelphia in 1757 he began to practice law, and by the time of his marriage to Mary Norris in 1770 he was one of the city's leading lawyers and something of a celebrity. His opposition to the Stamp Act resulted in the publication in 1768 of his *Letters From a Farmer in Pennsylvania to the Inhabitants of the British Colonies*, which articulated the colonists' sentiments about taxation without representation.

preceding pages

This mahogany sofa in the parlor of Poplar Hall is probably of English origin. Inscribed on the frame "1771" and "Duryea," it has a history of ownership by several generations of the Breese family of Newport, Rhode Island, a provenance that reflects the close commercial, religious, and family associations between Philadelphia and Newport Quakers. In front of the sofa is a Pennsylvania mahogany table of about 1750 with a lift top that conceals a writing board. The back stool is a simpler version of the famous set of chairs at Cliveden, the Chew mansion in Germantown.

Between the windows at the left is a Pennsylvania walnut slant-front desk; its early date of around 1750 is suggested by the drawer arrangement and the brasses. Above it hangs a bracket clock originally owned by John Dickinson; its dial is inscribed by Thomas Wagstaff, a London clockmaker who dealt regularly with Philadelphia Quaker merchants. Transitional Chippendale walnut chairs of a style popular in Delaware about 1760 surround the mahogany tea table of the same date, probably Philadelphia, in the corner. The Pennsylvania mahogany dressing table of about 1760 has its skirt and knees carved with shells.

This view of the parlor shows the angled design of the back legs of the mahogany sofa.

196

The paneling in the dining room of Poplar Hall is from Cherbourg, built in the mid-eighteenth century and demolished about the time of the restoration of Poplar Hall. The enclosed stairway at the right, leading to the room above, is typical of Delaware architecture. In the cupboard are eighteenth-century blue-and-white Chinese export porcelains and a set of English pearlware plates that bear the Dickinson crest and the cipher of John Dickinson's younger brother Philemon Dickinson and his wife, Mary Cadwalader. Around the late-eighteenth-century Philadelphia table are three of a set of six Philadelphia mahogany ladderback chairs dating from about 1790, which are of a type known to have been made by Jacob Wayne, a Philadelphia cabinetmaker.

The Coppock Great Hall of a Delaware River valley house is so called because all the paneling in the room, except the wainscoting, is from the Great Hall of the Bartholomew Coppock–James Bartram–Maris–West House. (The wainscoting is from a house in Manheim, Pennsylvania.) The ball-footed Pennsylvania walnut chest of drawers of around 1720 has a history of ownership in the Bonsall family, early settlers of Chester County. On it are two fine and rare examples of early English delftware—a posset pot of around 1660 and a porringer of about 1675—and a sixteenth-century English bronze candlestick with a central drip pan. The walnut-and-pine Pennsylvania hanging cupboard dates from the early eighteenth century, as does the walnut-and-pine candlestand made in Willistown, Chester County, which retains its original brownish paint. Silhouetted in the foreground is the crest rail and back of a very rare sassafras side chair of about 1730, made in the region of Naaman's Creek, Delaware, an early Swedish settlement on the Delaware River near the Pennsylvania border.

The walnut wainscot armchair of around 1750, in the Coppock Great Hall, descended in the Rodney family of Delaware to Caesar Rodney, the Kent County, Delaware, statesman and a signer of the Declaration of Independence. The small Pennsylvania walnut table beside it dates from the first quarter of the eighteenth century. On the Pennsylvania table of around 1720 in the foreground are a brass fat lamp set on a walnut base in the shape of a bell-bottomed candlestick, about 1735, made at Ephrata Cloister; a polychrome Delft charger, 1680–1700; a Liverpool delftware puzzle jug of about 1740; a late-eighteenth-century English hourglass; and early-eighteenth-century English wrought-iron tobacco tongs. The seventeen-arm chandelier of iron and maple stained red was made in New England around 1765. The walnut wainscot side chair on the left was made in Waynesboro, Pennsylvania, about 1750. The English cast-iron fireback depicting the Nativity is dated 1661, the approximate date of the English iron-and-brass-capped andirons.

The paneling in the living room of a Delaware River valley house comes from the early-eighteenth-century Colonel Benjamin Brannan House, which once stood in Darby, Pennsylvania. The paneling exemplifies the simple sophistication of many Philadelphia interiors. In front of the fireplace is a handsome Pennsylvania walnut fire screen–candlestand, about 1740, and a commodious English mahogany easy chair of about 1770. In front of the Philadelphia mahogany sofa of about the same date is an early-eighteenth-century maple tea table made in the Portsmouth, New Hampshire, region.

At the right of the sofa is a curly maple dressing table, about 1730, whose scalloped skirt and Spanish feet proclaim its Delaware River valley origin. Above it hangs a Queen Anne looking glass that bears the label of John Elliott Sr. and descended in the Wistar family of Philadelphia. The portrait of Sir Paul Pindar, painted in England in 1695, is by an unidentified artist. The walnut tall-case clock was made about 1765 in Philadelphia by Benjamin Rittenhouse, and the mahogany candlestand of about 1760 in the foreground was made in Lancaster, Pennsylvania.

Among several outstanding examples of early Pennsylvania joinery in the Coppock Great Hall is the handsome walnut wainscot armchair made in Philadelphia in the early eighteenth century. It and the red-oak side chair against the wall (signed by John Nash, a joiner working in Philadelphia in the first quarter of the eighteenth century) both came from the collection of Charles L. Hamilton, an enthusiastic early collector of Pennsylvania furniture. The substantial walnut chest of drawers, retaining its original finish, is signed by the Philadelphia joiner William Beake Jr. and is dated 1711. On it are a pair of English mid-seventeenth-century brass candlesticks and a Bristol delftware posset pot, 1700–1720. Above hangs an English walnut looking glass flanked by portraits of Jeremiah Theus and his wife in their original frames. The walnut table in the corner was made in Philadelphia about 1750 and supports a walnut Chester County spice chest of similar date.

The wall cupboard in the living room of a Delaware River valley house displays a sampling of Dutch and English delftware from the late seventeenth and early eighteenth centuries. The Lambeth plate at the left on the second shelf down, initialed "S*S/1734," is believed to have belonged originally to Thomas and Sarah Baker Smedley of Allistown, Pennsylvania. On the third shelf down are three so-called calendar plates made by Adriaen Kocks in Delft, 1686–1701. Seven plates from the original set of twelve, each representing a month, were brought by Vincent Loockerman from New York City to Dover, Delaware, in 1745. Two important examples of dated Bristol delftware are the Katherine Richards plate, dated 1742, in the center of the second shelf from the top and the plate in the middle of the bottom shelf, painted blue on a manganese ground, inscribed "R/NV/1739" on the obverse.

202

opposite page

The walnut gateleg table in the dining room in a Delaware River valley house was made in Philadelphia early in the eighteenth century. On it are a Bristol delftware bowl, 1730–40, and several examples of late-seventeenth- and early-eighteenth-century English brass. The so-called Boston chair of about 1740 has a history of ownership in the Ten Eyck family of Hurley, New York; it is one of an assembled set of eight side chairs and one armchair. The corner cupboard was salvaged from a house in Cheltenham, Pennsylvania, built by Tobias Leech, a wealthy miller who supplied his friend William Penn with sea biscuits for Penn's return visits to England. To the right of the cupboard is a Hudson River valley candlestand of about 1735 with its original stained black finish. The painted, paneled blanket chest is one of three known examples made of longleaf pine in Salem, New Jersey, around 1730. Above it hangs a portrait of an unidentified boy attributed to Gustavus Hesselius, believed to have been painted in the middle colonies.

View of the Wick House, Jockey Hollows, Morristown, New Jersey, built about 1750. The one-story frame-with-shingles structure served as Major General Arthur St. Clair's headquarters in the bitter winter of 1779–80, when Washington ordered his troops to winter quarters at Morristown for a second time. Nothing in the history of the trials of the Continental army, not even the ordeal at Valley Forge, compares to the cold white crucible of that second winter at Morristown. It was so cold that New York Harbor froze over. Howling blizzards lashed Morristown. Officers as well as men were often buried beneath deep drifts after the wind had blown their ragged tents away. Other soldiers, without tents or blankets, barefoot and half-naked, struggled to build rude huts out of the oak and maple trees around them. "We have never experienced a like extremity at any period of the war," Washington wrote, and soon he was complaining that his men lived off "every kind of horse food but hay."

THE SOUTHERN COLONIES:
THE MATURING OF SOCIETY AND CULTURE

Perilous Beginning:

Dawn and Morning Star

About the middle of May, 1607, three small ships under the command of Captain Christopher Newport sailed up the James River and anchored off a grassy and wooded peninsula. The vessels brought emigrants from England who would try once more to set up a colony in North America. The men who came with Captain Newport, a few more than a hundred, were weary with the long voyage, which had begun on the Thames the previous December. The earth of Virginia looked good to them; indeed, any solid ground would have been a relief, but Virginia in May was especially promising. Wild plums were in bloom and the sailors reported that strawberries crushed under their feet as they came ashore—surely an auspicious beginning for the settlement, named Jamestown in honor of their king.

Captain Newport and his companions came to the Chesapeake little prepared for what they found and with few qualifications for settling a raw wilderness. No Englishman had explored or mapped the great bay and its tributaries, and no one had described its natural features in any detail. What the settlers thought they knew of the region was grounded largely in the ignorance that flowed from the pens of promoters and explorers. Virginia was invariably depicted in fabulous language as a new Eden, peopled by natives who were alternately simple and friendly or cunning and dangerous, but always savage.

The Virginia adventurers had not come to plant a new nation; their object was much more modest and prosaic: they intended to explore the country, build a fort, seize whatever wealth was there, and hurry home. When Captain Newport sailed back for England he carried a letter from those left behind asking for reinforcements and supplies to keep the "all devouring Spaniards," as they described them, from laying "ravenous hands upon these gold showing mountains." Unruly and not given to hard work, the Virginia settlers were soon whipped into shape by Captain John Smith, who took command after Newport's departure. They learned that they had to work with their hands or perish, but they did not learn without quarrel or protest. Nevertheless, by the time winter had come they had cut trees, erected mud and wattle houses, and begun to make bricks for a church and other permanent structures. Captain Smith explored the countryside and traded with the Indians; had it not been for the corn which he obtained by barter, the colonists would have fared ill that first winter. The next winter, which has gone down in history as the "starving time," was much worse. The men started to sicken and die so quickly, as John Smith later remembered, "that the living were scarce able to bury the dead." The dying continued and when Newport returned with more supplies and settlers, only thirty-eight men were still alive.

One may wonder that the English starved in the midst of abundance. But these were for the most part city people from London. They had no capacity to adapt themselves to conditions and no equipment for, or skill in, fishing or hunting; they were about as ill prepared as colonists have ever been. Smith acknowledged as much when he wrote the Virginia Company in 1608, "though there be fish in the Sea, foules in the ayre, and Beasts in the woods, their bounds are so large, they are so wild, and we so weake and ignorant, we cannot much trouble them." By May 1610, of the 500 colonists who had been alive in the fall, a mere sixty embittered and discouraged survivors, ready to give up and return to England, remained.

The colony survived, but it found no gold in the nearby hills. The backers of the venture, the Virginia Company of London, made no money out of the enterprise, largely because of the lack of any product which could be turned quickly and profitably into money. The Virginians were not able to develop satisfactory trade with the Indians, and their first attempts at farming were not successful. But about 1612, John Rolfe discovered that tobacco could be grown easily and would sell for a high price. The successful cultivation of tobacco—from West Indian and Orinoco plants, not the strong and bitter Virginia weed used by the Indians—produced exports of about 50,000 pounds in 1618, a figure that rose more than sixfold by 1626. Englishmen had a fondness for tobacco; the attraction of the weed had grown steadily ever since smoking had taken the fancies of the fashionable back in the 1580s. In 1577 an Englishman named John Frampton wrote *Joyful News Out of the New Found World* devoted to a description of the virtues of tobacco, and many doctors believed it to be a remedy for almost any ailment, from gunshot wounds to epilepsy.

Tobacco planting quickly became the colonists' chief occupation, and it sustained the colony during its early years. Every available acre, including the streets of Jamestown, was sown with tobacco as hopeful and greedy planters neglected other crops. Within a generation tobacco became the primary crop and was cultivated on a commercial scale—dooming the emerging colonial society to a single-crop economy dependent on bound laborers. In the half century after 1625 the cultivation and marketing of tobacco became the colonists' economic lifeblood. Trade in the weed provided colonists with things they were incapable of manufacturing for themselves, and in an economy where hard currency was always scarce, tobacco became the medium for exchanging goods and services.

Other things were happening in the small colony in these early years. The first representative assembly met in the church at Jamestown on July 30, 1619, the only building large enough to accommodate the governor, his six councillors, and the twenty elected representatives, known as burgesses. Their meeting was momentous, for it set a precedent for self-government and representative political institutions in Virginia and elsewhere in colonial America. From this time on, Virginians jealously guarded their right to make their own laws. Plans for schools and a university were also made, although the actual founding of the school received a setback in the great Indian massacre of 1622, when 347 settlers—a third of the colony's population—were killed in one day. Once the colonists recovered from their shock and disarray, they retaliated, and both sides settled down to a brutal war of attrition that dragged on sporadically until the late 1620s. The war took its toll in more than lives and property—it also

helped to bring down the Virginia Company, whose charter was voided in 1624. Following the unexpected death of James in March 1625, the new monarch, Charles I, proclaimed Virginia a royal colony.

Fabulous expectations, inadequate capitalization, inept colonists, divided government, incompetent leadership, and loss of will all contributed to the bankruptcy and failure of the Virginia Company. Yet even in loss there was benefit. The early settlers taught future colonists practical lessons about the New World. Despite hardships and suffering, the English gained a toehold in North America, ultimately leading to the creation of an empire. They grew tobacco and raised foodstuffs for their households, and the door was opened to the future economic and social development of Virginia. In time they developed a civilization and transplanted the best of the British tradition and bequeathed an enduring legacy of social values, government, liberty, and law.

First Families and a Half-Century of Growth:
Planters and Gentlemen

Virginia in 1675 only faintly resembled the place that Charles I had proclaimed a Crown colony half a century earlier. From the eastern shore across the Chesapeake Bay to the fall line, scattered communities of settlers and tobacco fields replaced Indian villages and virgin land. Gone were the early adventurers who viewed their sojourn in the wilderness as temporary. In their stead came immigrants who intended to stay; their commitment to prospering in the New World gave shape and substance to Virginia society. The nearly formless government of the Virginia Company gave way to distinct provincial and local governing institutions, a body of indigenous law, and a discernible political structure. Virginia had changed from a tenuous colonial outpost to something much closer to its English antecedents.

Apart from a few thousand Africans and an even smaller contingent of continental Europeans, Virginia was settled by Englishmen. The customs, language, and law of the Old Dominion, as Virginia came to be known, were English in origin, and non-English immigrants would be compelled to take on the ways

206

of transplanted Englishmen. The English that Virginia attracted were a special type, and they left an indelible stamp on the social order they created. Like their countrymen at home, they presumed a stratified society that fit everyone into a hierarchy of vocations ranging from the monarch to the lowliest subject. Although rigid, these graduations were not inflexible, and upward mobility—through commerce, the church, the law, the military, or service to the monarch—was possible.

All of England sent settlers to Virginia, but the earliest came from the West Country around Bristol. In the colony's formative years, the rural Bristol gentry sent many young offshoots to Virginia; the crop failures and decline in West Country mining and manufacture were great incentives. In the 1660s Virginia also attracted many loyalists, or Cavaliers, from northern England, who named their Northern Neck counties for the Lancaster, Northumberland, and Westmoreland they left behind. Settlers from East Anglian counties such as Norfolk, Suffolk, Essex, and Kent were also drawn to the colony. The bulk of immigrants came from what Stuart Englishmen called "the middling sort," whose standing ranged from near poverty to near greatness. They were yeomen, husbandmen, craftsmen, and the younger progeny of substantial mercantile families.

Some farmers rose from the yeomen's ranks through hard work and the acquisition of land. Others came to Virginia equipped with wealth and education. The great planters took up strategically sited land along the riverfronts, building their houses near the landing places. The humbler yeomen and tenants set up their homes away from the main waterways, so the majority of the population lived amid fields and trees along the lesser creeks. In 1724 the Reverend Mr. Hugh Jones described the domestic architecture of the Virginia settlements in his *The Present State of Virginia:* "The gentlemen's seats are of late built for the most part of good brick . . . commodious, and capacious . . . the common planters live in pretty timber houses, neater than the farm houses are generally in England . . . with timber also are built houses for the overseers . . . The Negros live in small cottages called quarters, in about six in a gang, under the direction of an overseer."

The common Virginia house was a one- or one-and-a-half-story timber-frame dwelling with two rooms on the ground floor and a chimney on the gable at one or both ends. The dwellings,

like the fields, often bore the marks of the constant need of tobacco growers and tenants to relocate. In 1784 J. F. D. Smyth in his *Tour in the United States of America* noted that "the houses here are almost all of wood, covered with the same; the roof with shingles, the sides and ends with thin boards, and not always lathed and plastered within; only those of the better sort are finished in that manner, and painted on the outside. The chimneys are sometimes of brick, but more commonly of wood, coated on the inside with clay. The windows of the best sort have glass in them; the rest have none, and only wooden shutters."

The houses of the common planters ranged in form and degree of finish from disciplined rectangularity to makeshift irregularity, and the overall impression of the farmhouses and farms was not one of extreme orderliness. The natural abundance of well-watered land, where horses, cattle, and hogs could range freely, did not encourage intensive use of space or the strict cultivation of crops. Travelers noted that orchards flourished, but they implied no careful ordering of the landscape when they observed that Virginians "plant them . . . in the worst of their ground in order to Improve it, their Cattle and Swine feeding under [the trees]." "The Fruit-Trees are wonderfully quick of growth," noted Robert Beverley in *The History and Present State of Virginia* in 1705, "so that in six or seven years time from the Planting, a Man may bring an Orchard to bear in great plenty, from which he may make store of good Cyder, Or distill great quantities of Brandy . . . Yet they have very few that take any care at all for an Orchard; nay, many . . . let them go to ruine, and expose the Trees to be torn, and barked by the Cattle." Worm fences, zigzag stacks of split young tree trunks, lacked the rectilinear precision of posts and rails; "making Virginia fences" became a metaphor for inebriation.

Virginian houses were filled with an array of furniture and personal belongings that varied according to the householder's wealth. Some got by with little more than modest furnishings, a few cooking utensils, and the essential tools. More affluent householders stuffed their living quarters with beds, tables, chairs, chests, pots, pans, and dishes, linens, and even silverware. Items the colonists could not manufacture or obtain readily in Virginia, like weapons, flocked mattresses, edge tools, and cast-iron pots, were highly valued and often willed to a favorite relative. Clothing varied as much as household furnishings: it was a badge of one's social distinction as much as protection against the elements. Clothing items were made to last, and like the pewter porringer or musket, were passed from generation to generation until they wore out.

The Backcountry:

The Sweetest Part of This Country

The western movement of Chesapeake society began in the late seventeenth century, as venturesome people passed beyond the fall line onto the Piedmont plateau, clearing lands for tobacco and organizing local governments authorized by the assemblies. Between 1732 and the outbreak of the Revolution, Virginia established twenty-one new counties east of the Blue Ridge, of which fifteen, together with five new Shenandoah Valley counties, comprised the Old Dominion's portion of the backcountry. Spilling down the Great Wagon Road that traversed the Great Valley of Virginia, the enormous flood of new settlers had inundated the northern reaches of the valley by the 1730s and had reached the Yadkin River valley of North Carolina before the end of the 1740s. From Virginia and North Carolina they spread out to South Carolina, Tennessee, and Kentucky.

The massive migration from Europe and Britain that led to the settlement of the backcountry had begun early in the seventeenth century. The Presbyterian lowland Scots transported to northern Ireland early in that century were soon harassed by the Anglican High Church and were denied both civil and religious rights under the Test Act of 1704. Outrageous feudal quitrents, a failing economy, and the famine of the 1720s drove the Scotch-Irish to America: 6,000 settled in Pennsylvania in 1729 alone. Germans and Swiss fared no better in their homelands. Long residents of an international buffer zone, the peasants of the Rhenish Palatinate suffered during the 1688–97 War of the League of Augsburg and then during the War of Spanish Succession, which began in 1702. By 1708 shiploads of German immigrants were arriving daily in Philadelphia. French Huguenots, who fled the continent in great numbers after the revocation of the Edict of Nantes in 1685, found their way to American coastal communities and the backcountry.

The awesome expanse of the interior regions of the southern backcountry, geographically split by the Appalachians and a system of deep rivers, was settled by the "dregs and gleanings" of other English colonies, a populace that was scarcely governable until after the Revolution. The interior parts of North Carolina were reputed to be a place where debtors, thieves, and vagabonds might flee to because of a colonial law that protected settlers from foreign debts. In 1730, there were between 30,000 and 35,000 people in the colony—predominantly English, with elements of Welsh, French, German Palatines, and Scotch-Irish. In 1750, there were between 65,000 and 75,000; and by 1770 immigration had swelled the number to somewhere between 175,000 and 185,000.

The inland parts were very different from the maritime regions, a fact that was soon recognized by early travelers and visitors. John Lawson's extensive travels in North Carolina were recorded in *A New Voyage to Carolina* (1709): "It must be confessed that the most noble and sweetest Part of this Country is not inhabited by any but the Savages; and a great deal of the richest Part thereof, has no Inhabitants but the Beasts of the Wilderness . . . near the Mountains, you meet with the richest Soil, a sweet, thin Air, dry Roads, pleasant small murmuring Streams, and several beneficial Productions and Species, which are unknown in the European World."

The movement of settlers into the North Carolina backcountry was so conspicuous in the 1750s that it aroused much comment. In 1754, the governor told the Board of Trade that settlers were coming in from the north in hundreds of wagons. A minister writing from Virginia in 1756 reported that 300 Virginians en route to North Carolina passed Bedford courthouse in one week, that between January and October of 1755, 5,000 had crossed the James River bound for North Carolina, and that great numbers were following each day. If these figures were not always accurate, they at least give some impression of the magnitude of the movement. Other southern colonies, such as Georgia, were also experiencing large increases, but North Carolina's Governor Tryon was not wrong when, in 1766, he boasted that his colony was being settled faster than any on the continent. A newspaper report from Williamsburg, Virginia, in 1767, marveled at the incoming waves of settlers: "There is scarce any history, either ancient or modern, which affords an account of such a rapid and sudden increase of inhabitants in a back frontier country, as that of North Carolina. To justify the truth of this observation, we need only to inform our readers, that twenty years ago there were not twenty taxable persons with the limits of the County of Orange; in which there are now four thousand taxables. The increase of inhabitants, and flourishing state of the other adjoining back counties, are no less surprising and astonishing."

Most of the Scotch-Irish coming to North Carolina made the journey overland, chiefly from colonies to the north and particularly from Pennsylvania, where many had disembarked. The exodus of Scottish Highlanders to the colony began after the Treaty of Union in 1707, grew in volume as a "spirit of emigration" became common, and reached a peak shortly before the Revolution. By 1775 there were perhaps as many as 10,000 Highlanders in the colony; almost all of them came across the Atlantic Ocean directly to North Carolina. After landing near the mouth of the Cape Fear River, they moved inland into a fairly compact region that straddled the eastern and western parts of the south-central section of the colony. There were also some Scottish Lowlanders, few in number by comparison with the Highlanders but important because they included a small group of merchants who played a leading role in the economic development of the colony. Englishmen also came into the colony, by both land and sea, and they scattered into all parts of it.

German-speaking peoples constituted the other major element in the backcountry. The Germans were of different Protestant denominations, of which Lutheran, Moravian, and Reformed were the most common, and came originally from different parts of Europe. Despite their different places of origin, the Germans were generally considered by others as a distinct group and they regarded themselves as a separate and distinctive fraternity. Most of the Germans who entered the colony came overland from the north on the Great Wagon Road. After following the Shenandoah Valley through most of north and central Virginia, the road led east through the Staunton River gap of the Blue Ridge, and then turned south; it crossed the Dan River in North Carolina and reached the Yadkin River in the vicinity of the Moravian tract. Other roads extended from the Yadkin through the town of Salisbury and into South Carolina.

The German elements tended to concentrate in cliquish German areas. One German minister, writing home from one of the more exclusively German settlements in western North Carolina, expressed the somewhat antagonistically detached German identity in the New World: "Among the things to be especially emphasized for the younger people . . . was the admonishment not to contract any marriages with the English or the Irish. And even though this may seem very unreasonable to a European, it is in this region a very important matter. For in the first place, the Irish in this section are lazy, dissipated and poor, live in the most wretched huts and enjoy the same food as their animals . . . In the second place, it is very seldom that German and English blood is happily united in wedlock. Dissensions and feeble children are often the result. The English wife will not permit her husband to be master in his household, and when he likewise insists upon his rights crime and murder ensue. In the third place, the English of this region do not adhere to any definite religion, do hot have their children christened; nor do they send them to any school, but simply let them grow up like domestic animals."

"An American," the anonymous author of *American Husbandry*, summed up his 1775 account of the differences between North Carolina's interior and maritime: "In a word, all the necessaries and many of the luxuries of life abound in the back parts of this province, which, with the temperate climate, renders it one of the finest countries in America; so fine, that every body must be astonished at finding any settlements made on the unhealthy sea coast, which is nearly the reverse." He strongly recommended that new settlers fix themselves upon the hitherto neglected back parts of the country, for "every reason of effect conspires to show the propriety of settling the back parts of this province in preference to the maritime ones." But these late recommendations were superfluous. By 1775, settlers had already discovered the attractions of the back parts, and during the previous twenty or thirty years had been flocking into the area in large numbers.

The Riches of the Carolina Low Country:

The Unbought Graces of Life

For half a century after the first settlement of 1670, South Carolina was a buffer province, walled in on the south and west by the Spanish and Indians. With the establishment in 1732 of Georgia as a barrier against the Spanish and a concurrent growth in rice culture, Carolina society came out of its infancy and began to assume a definite regional form. Eventually it took in the plantation country on either side of the Savannah River and on the Georgia Sea Islands as far south as St. Simon's; it also spread northward along the coast past the mouth of the Peden after 1735. About this time, too, newly arrived immigrants pushed inland from Charles Town up the courses of the Santee and Edisto rivers, to a district where they founded townships; by 1750 these areas were regarded as part of the Low Country.

All avenues in the Low Country, by sea or by land, led to the southern metropolis of Charles Town. Although founded in 1670 and moved to its present location in 1680, Charles Town did not begin to grow amazingly until the 1730s. (Charles Town became Charleston in 1783, when the town was incorporated as a city.) Located between two estuarial rivers, the Ashley and the Cooper, and close to two others, the Stono and Wands, it was situated in such a way that it would profit as soon as the surrounding country produced commodities for export. Charles Town also had more extensive connections to the interior than neighboring towns, by way of the old Indian path to the Cherokee country and by the famous wagon road from Charles Town to Philadelphia. As the capital of South Carolina, its military headquarters, and the sole seat of provincial justice before 1759, the bustling little metropolis was the focus of the entire economic and political life of Carolina society.

Charles Town was the hub of the Low Country, giving Carolina society its commercial connections with the rest of the world. In addition to handling the plantation trade, Charles Town was also the center of Indian traffic in deerskins. The overland trade routes brought 50,000 deerskins annually to Charles Town from the Indian nations, and as trade in rice and indigo expanded, the inland waterways also became major avenues to market. After 1750 an extensive wagon trade also developed between the backcountry and Charles Town, as settlers brought increasing amounts of wheat, flour, and pork in exchange for manufactured goods.

Charles Town's commerce was supported by three crops—first rice, then indigo, and finally sea island cotton—and also supplemented by naval stores. Although rice was introduced in the 1690s, the clearing of swamps and the diking of marshes took many years, as did the effort to produce the best seeds and to find a suitable labor force. A profitable market for rice was beginning to develop in both the Mediterranean and northern Europe, and it was made an enumerated commodity in 1703, which meant that it could not be shipped directly to foreign markets. But this restriction was lifted in 1731, and the trade picked up enormously. Production, which rose from 10,000 to 100,000 barrels between 1720 and 1760, was boosted by the expansion of cultivation to the adjacent areas of North Carolina and Georgia, and by 1760 rice accounted for about twenty percent of colonial commodity exports.

The onerous cultivation of rice demanded intensive labor, a demand met by increasing numbers of black slaves. The crop encouraged the use of slaves for two reasons: First, laborers working cooperatively in groups of five or ten were more efficient than an individual farmer aided by his immediate family. Second, the miasmic coastal lowlands had a reputation as an unhealthful region teeming with a host of mysterious fevers. Whites often spent part of the year in Charles Town, hoping to escape the diseases associated with the swampy tidal rice fields.

Rice was a very profitable crop, and rice culture provided the setting for the emergence of a distinct economic and political elite—the planter class. Beginning in 1670 with a handful of Barbadian Goose Creek gentlemen, after 1730 it began to flower in wealth, prestige, and numbers. Families of actual gentle birth were few; the prosperous bourgeois of middle-class English and European origins, grown rich and seeking gentility, set the style. Due to the planters' dominance, the South mirrored more closely than the North the structure of English society. Yet unlike England, where the franchise was narrowly restricted, most small farmers in the colonies were eligible to vote, and in a deferential manner they elected wealthy neighbors who were well qualified to protect local interests. In the mother country, the landed gentry were primarily landlords who rented small farms to a large number of tenant families. Nonagricultural pursuits were considered socially degrading, and English landlords did not become extensively involved in mercantile activities. By contrast, the great planters of Carolina were deeply involved not only in the management of their estates but also in a wide range of complementary enterprises. Few southerners achieved great wealth through agriculture alone; the great planters were land developers, moneylenders, lawyers, and part-time merchants, engaging in any economic activity that promised to pay an adequate return.

In 1712, the Carolinas split into two colonies after a disastrous war with the Tuscarora Indians, and in 1729 both North and South Carolina passed into royal control after their English-based proprietors saw their powers whittled away and finally lost to the Crown. South Carolina rice cultivation spread north over the North Carolina boundary on the lower Cape Fear, and on the Albemarle Sound in the early eighteenth-century, a number of wealthy families associated with the Virginia gentry gained political status and considerable property. This social elite in the Albemarle and Cape Fear regions matured in the 1730s and 1740s, and the gentry from both areas began to intermarry.

From its beginnings, North Carolina was split into two halves, north and south. Albemarle Sound, at the northern reaches of the colony, was settled mainly by people from Virginia who produced tobacco, while to the south, Cape Fear was populated largely by rice farmers from South Carolina. Until the 1730s the northern counties dominated the legislature, but as the Cape Fear region expanded, it began to demand more representation and eventually the removal of the provincial capital from Edenton to New Bern. Following the selection of New Bern in 1765 as the site of the capital, Tryon's Palace was constructed, serving both as the governor's residence and the meeting place of the government.

Chartered in 1732, Georgia was the last of the British colonies in America to be founded by settlers coming directly from Europe. Although defense of the South Carolina frontier was one motive for bringing settlers to the area, James Oglethorpe and his philanthropic friends in England wished to use the new colony as a haven for debtors languishing in English prisons. Once the colony's charter was issued, the original concern for debtors disappeared, and the trustees sought to persuade small tradesmen and artisans to emigrate and become, according to the trustees, "a self-sufficient peasantry raising silk and wine." But these dreams were thwarted by the actual conditions among the mosquito-ridden cypress swamps of the Altamaha River. Georgia did not quickly flourish, and the poorly organized government of the trustees finally surrendered Georgia to the Crown in 1752.

Georgia's early inhabitants looked to the example of South Carolina for the path to wealth. Influential men claimed that the restrictions on the size of land grants and on the use of slaves inhibited Georgia's prosperity; in response to their agitation the land grant restrictions were set aside in 1740, and in 1750 the antislave law was repealed. While Georgia below the Altamaha remained a frontier for many years, around Savannah slavery, rice growing, and large landholdings rapidly transformed the area into a recognizable Southern society, which by 1775 had a population of about 24,000 whites and 15,000 slaves. Georgia also benefited from the removal of the French from the Ohio, the crushing of the Indians, and the removal of the Spanish from the South, and the aristocracy was soon expressing great self-confidence and assertiveness. Peace, prosperity, and sustained economic growth blessed the colony's first forty years, and as 1775 opened, the colony, far from the political turmoil of the North, had little reason to suspect that economic progress would not continue.

The Carolina Low Country soon developed the familiar hierarchy of classes and offered magnificent opportunities for men of enterprise. After 1730 prosperity seemed endemic, as riches amassed in trade were plowed back onto profit-yielding rice and indigo fields. As if to compensate for the rawness of a youthful society, the size of the fortunes accumulated in the Carolina Low Country exceeded those known elsewhere in British America. Henry Middleton, for example, possessed an estate of 50,000 acres and 800 slaves, and in 1751 the British House of Commons was told that Daniel Huger "is now, and long has been, possessed of eight thousand pounds old South Sea annuities."

This expanding society necessarily took to building permanent dwellings, and the region's riches found their most conspicuous form in the planters' great houses. During the five years preceding 1773, over three hundred houses, many of them elegant, were built along the Bay, the Ashley, and in the White Point and Ansonborough sections of Charles Town. The Charles

Town single house and double house became justly famous. The single house, which takes its name from its one-room width, became the unique Charles Town house and provided a practical solution to the problem of keeping cool. The building stands with its gable-end to the street and consists, typically, of two rooms on a floor, with a hall between containing the staircase, while a piazza runs along one side of the house (generally the south or west) to shelter it from the sun and to provide outdoor living space. The entrance is usually through the piazza, which may present a false door to the street. The double house was English in form and design, copied from an architect's pattern book, and sometimes modified by a gentleman architect or master housewright, and adapted to local conditions.

These houses and many handsome new public edifices, such as St. Michael's Church, the State House, the Exchange, and the Theater, as well as wide streets and fine gardens, produced an appearance of beauty and dignity which evoked admiration and comment from newcomers. Indeed, Elkanah Watson asserted that "perhaps no city of America exhibits, in proportion to its size, so much splendor and style." The cool and airy high-ceilinged interiors of the great town houses were elaborately decorated and elegantly furnished according to the latest London fashions, and were designed to be seen best when their owners entertained— which was often.

The pursuit of pleasure took many forms in Charleston society. After wining and dining at the mid-afternoon dinner, numerous attractions drew a Carolina gentleman forth for the remainder of the day, and often much of the night. Recreation and diversions of all kinds were highly organized; clubs and private societies existed for almost any reason, and most gentlemen belonged to several. There was a Whist Club as early as 1732, and in succeeding years the city hosted convivial gatherings with such strange names as the Fort Jolly Volunteers, Smoking Club, Meddlers, Beef-Steak Club, Laughing Club, and the Fancy Society. In addition, there were clubs designed for some specific purpose or worthy cause, including a Masonic lodge formed in 1735 and the St. Cecilia Society, founded in 1735, which held concerts. Charles Town also had a symphony orchestra, two fine theater orchestras, a chorus for the opera, and excellent singers. For those interested in out-of-door diversions, fowling and hunting offered great sport.

In the 1730s cockfighting was the rage, champion cocks being taken to any parish to meet a challenger. But horse racing took precedence a few years later, when Thomas Nightingale opened the Newmarket Course on Charleston Neck in 1754, and in 1758 the sport of kings was firmly established with the founding of the Carolina Jockey Club. Race week in February became the most important week of the year for society; planters and their families flocked to Charles Town for a round of balls and parties. Of course, there were also detractors; J. Hector St. John de Crèvecoeur thought that "the rays of their sun seems to urge them irresistibly to dissipation and pleasure." Yankee Josiah Quincy was more precise in his censure: "Cards, dice, the bottle and horse engross prodigious portions of time and attention: the gentlemen (planters and merchants) are mostly men of the turf and gamesters."

Although amusements were plentiful, intellectual life in Carolina society was scarce. "Literature is in its infancy here," Governor William Bull advised the Board of Trade in 1770. "Of Arts and Sciences we have only such branches as serve the necessities, the conveniences and the comforts of man. The more refined such as serve to adorn or minister to the luxuries of life are as yet little known here." The Charles Town Library Society, formed in 1748 by seventeen citizens, hoping "to save their descendants from sinking into savagery," facilitated the development of a taste for reading. The Library Society never attained the scientific and educational objectives of its founders, but by 1770 it had a collection of nearly 2,000 books. The printing presses of Charles Town also played a significant role in dispensing useful knowledge to the Low Country. In 1732 Lewis Timothy, with Benjamin Franklin's support, began publication of the region's first newspaper, the *South-Carolina Gazette*.

If literature and science were denied the encouragement and support of the gentry, this was not the case with the polite arts. The residents generously subscribed to theaters and concerts, and the *South-Carolina Gazette* boasted in 1774 that "many Gentlemen of Taste and Fortune are giving the utmost encouragement to Architecture." But the Revolution was disruptive of the intellectual achievements of the city. Some of the leading scholars and intellectuals became loyalists and took the king's side. And the Library Society and the Charles Town Museum suffered severe losses in the fire of 1778, which destroyed 6,000 to 7,000 books, paintings, prints, mathematical instruments, and a pair of elegant globes.

Charles Town was like Humphrey Clinker's London, "the great wen" that drained the vigor from the rural areas. Yet it provided a vision of the elegant life, elevated above the common sphere. The rich planters displayed and consumed their wealth in the most lavish way possible, but it was not the grasping materialism of vulgarity and grossness. Rather, it was wealth circumscribed by a powerful aristocratic tradition, with a scrupulous standard of taste, an explicit standard of honorable occupations, and a rigid standard of prestige. This was the only leisure-class society in colonial British America, the only people among whom "the unbought graces of life"—enjoyment, charm, refinement—became the summum bonum.

The Golden Age of Colonial Chesapeake Society:

Enlightenment, Tobacco, and Slaves

By the second quarter of the eighteenth century, the Tidewater economy was on the verge of a takeoff that would last until the American Revolution. With increasing wealth, the provinces of Maryland and Virginia came into their own. A small and increasingly cosmopolitan planter elite dominated the society and found themselves part of the British Enlightenment, to a much greater extent than anyone could have envisioned just a few decades before. Below the elite existed a large number of middling planters and yeoman farmers, bound to the elite in many ways, not least by their shared status as landowners, tobacco planters, and slaveholders. Together they formed a stable, integrated social order, an order that found concrete form in county courts, militia musters, and parish churches.

The fundamental force behind the golden era of Chesapeake society was the expanding economy. The opening of the French market early in the eighteenth century brought renewed life to the tobacco industry, and diversification made the economy less dependent on a single crop. Planters added wheat and other grains to their crops, and produced cloth, leather, and metal products that earlier had been imported. Local markets began to develop and

over time the economy became more diversified and stable. But tobacco growing remained the underpinning of Chesapeake society. After a tobacco-industry recession that lasted from 1680 to 1720, production increased phenomenally. By 1740 Chesapeake tobacco exports equaled the combined volume of all the world's tobacco-growing regions. This increased production did not involve any improvement in techniques; on the contrary, even the most elementary corrections to the faulty agriculture were long in coming. The planters' habits had been formed in a land of gentle rainfall and mainly tough soils, but the Chesapeake saw clouds pile high, the heavens crash, and rain fall in torrents on light, easily eroded soils. Leaching of the soil by floods compounded the depletion worked by the tobacco plant, greedy for potash and nitrogen. Only the importation of more labor and the opening up of new land permitted greater production.

The luster of this golden era rested on an extraordinarily high level of exploitation—particularly in the form of black slavery. Slavery in the Chesapeake was not the rigorous, regimented variety found in the Caribbean or even low country South Carolina, but it was nonetheless dependent, like all slave systems, on brute force. Chesapeake planters imported over 100,000 Africans between 1700 and 1770, and the slave population grew from 13,000 to 250,000 in the same period. Because demand became greater than could be supplied from the West Indies, through which most earlier slaves had passed, after 1720 virtually all came directly from Africa. About twenty percent of the Africans died from the rigors of the ocean voyage—the infamous Middle Passage—during which they were packed for weeks between decks too close for standing; probably twenty-five percent more died during "seasoning," their transition into slavery. Survivors found little to ameliorate their condition in the New World. Family life was uncommon, for as might be expected among persons selected for heavy labor, males predominated by more than two to one. Although almost two-thirds came from the same region of Africa, there were still, in Hugh Jones's words, so many "harsh jargons" among them that many were foreigners to each other. Loneliness and despair were the reaction of many new arrivals to their fate.

The settlement of the Piedmont and the valley in Virginia led to a great surge in agricultural production. Rapid expansion to the west was encouraged by a new philosophy of land grants, which were now issued before the settlers came, conditioning title upon the seating of a certain number of persons within a specified time. From tens of thousands of acres, grants escalated to more than 100,000 acres. This policy carried the plantation system into most corners of the colony, continuing and spreading the trend toward social stratification that had begun in the previous century. In areas where land had been distributed in large tracts, new arrivals became tenants—there was almost no other way to settle.

The traditional English culture so admired by the American gentry rested on a patronage society of personal influence and dependent relationships in a carefully ordered world. This society was structured like a pyramid, with subtly arranged degrees of ranks running from the king and nobles at the pinnacle to bound laborers at the base. Each place in the social hierarchy carried with it obligations and responsibilities to ranks above and below. Speech, deportment, manners, and dress revealed station in society, as clearly as did liveried equipment, the size and splendor of the home, and the quantity and quality of food consumed by the household. The nobility displayed distinctive badges and honors of place, the gentry exhibited coats of arms, and those of the middle ranks, lower orders, and the laboring poor wore clothing appropriate to their position.

The British Enlightenment reached its height in the eighteenth century, and Virginia shared, albeit tangentially, in its triumphs. The age was characterized by a confident belief that the intellectual achievements of Europe were matched in Western civilization only by those of the ancient world. Knowledge of the classics was the first step in education. Every cultivated person was comfortable with the copious classical allusions and pithy quotations from Greek and Roman authors in the literature and speech of the time. But Tidewater society, still only a few miles removed from the untamed wilderness, lagged far behind British culture. Fashions and styles often came to the colonies ten to twenty years after they peaked in England. And as far as widespread education and betterment was concerned, Hugh Jones summed up the situation in 1724: "Virginians being naturally of good parts . . . neither require nor admire as much learning, as we do in Britain."

Tidewater Plantations and Georgian Houses:

Beautiful and Commodious, Adapted to the Nature of the Country

The most obvious sign of the golden era of Chesapeake society was the building of Georgian mansions along the rivers of the Tidewater. Awe-inspiring in their magnificence, they were symbols of the great planters' wealth and political and social authority. They were also intellectual statements, conscious testimony that the colony's leaders were abreast of the latest European ideas. In the maturing colonial society, Williamsburg, Virginia, became a jewel in the crown of the British empire. Robert Beverley wrote of the growing city in 1705, "There are two fine Public Buildings in this Country, which are the most Magnificent of any in America," the Capitol and the College. The Reverend Hugh Jones, writing twenty-five years after the city's founding, added the Palace to this list: "These buildings are justly reputed the best in all *English America*, and are exceeded by few of their kind in *England*."

As the Capitol rose and Williamsburg became a proper city and the capital of a strapping colony, lesser structures multiplied, raised by skilled men who borrowed design traditions from English architecture manuals. This vernacular architecture was a combination of English style and American substance: it joined English forms and traditions with native materials like "heart" pine, straight-grained and everlasting wood cut from the center of trees that had grown for centuries in the Tidewater's dense forests. "Here, as in other parts, they build with brick, but most commonly with timber," wrote Hugh Jones. "Cased with feather-edged plank, painted with white lead and oil, covered with shingles of cedar, etc. tarred over at first; with a passage generally through the middle of the house for an airdraught in summer. Thus their houses are lasting, dry, and warm in winter, and cool in summer; especially if there be windows enough to draw the air. Thus they dwell comfortably, genteely, pleasantly, and plentifully in this delightful, healthful, and (I hope) thriving city of Williamsburg."

Williamsburg architecture derived mainly from the same Palladian principles that informed New England architecture. The Georgian buildings followed rules of mathematical symmetry, reflecting both classical taste and the cult of Newtonian science that characterized the Enlightenment. Across town from the Capitol was the College, "beautiful and commodious, being first modeled by Sir Christopher Wren [and] adapted to the nature of the country," as Hugh Jones described it. In between lay Bruton Parish Church, "adorned as the best churches in London"; the Powder Magazine, "a large octagon tower"; and the debtors' prison, whose flat roof was an architectural first in Virginia. The pièce de resistance was the Palace, an archetype of the style; begun in 1705 and completed under Governor Spotswood in 1720, the scale and magnificence of the residence and its grounds revolutionized architectural thinking in Virginia.

Planters' mansions sprang up throughout the region, fitting monuments to the gentry's self-confidence and power. All of the grandest residences built in the colony in the decades after the Palace was completed were conceived upon Governor Spotswood's fundamental plan—a great house surrounded by clusters of dependencies, a layout given formal balance by the addition of adjoining "offices" symmetrically arranged on each side of the central block. A strong sense of dominance and submission was expressed in the elevation of a central unit from the subordinated elements, intensifying the view of the great house as a self-sufficient rural community. The new style spread throughout the colonies— notable examples include Robert Carter I's remodeled Corotoman in Lancaster County; Benjamin Harrison IV's Berkeley and William Byrd II's Westover in Charles City County; Thomas Lee's Stratford Hall and Robert Carter's II's Nomini Hall in Westmoreland; and in Chesterfield, Henry Cary's Ampthill. These country seats were identified with Roman villas such as Horace's Sabine farm, from which Landon Carter took the name of his newly built country seat, Sabine Hall, in Richmond County.

William Hugh Grove, an English traveler in 1732, recorded his first impressions of such houses: "I went by ship up the [York] river, which has pleasant Seats on the Bank which Shew Like little villages, for having Kitchins, Dayry houses, Barns, Stables, Store houses, and some of them 2 or 3 Negro Quarters all Separate from Each other but near the mansion houses . . . Most of These have pleasant Gardens and the Prospect of the River render them very pleasant [and] equall to the Thames from London to Richmond, supposing the Towns omitted." The Englishman noted that "they

have a broad Stayrcase with a passage thro the house in the middle, which is the Summer hall and Draws the air." Some houses had two rooms on each side of the passage; others, of more traditional design, had only one, "and the Windows opposite each other" for ventilation.

The increasingly self-confident Virginia gentry liked to think of their estates as retreats from a world of unworthy striving, where, as one declared, "we sit securely under our Vines and our Fig Trees." The biblical tone of this description also appears in William Byrd II's idyll on plantation life. In 1726, just as he was about to undertake the building of Westover, one of the most beautifully sited and executed of the great Tidewater houses, Byrd wrote: "I have a large Family of my own, and my Doors are open to Every Body, yet I have no Bills to pay, and half-a-Crown will rest undisturbed in my Pocket for many Moons. Like one of the Patriarchs, I have my Flocks and my Herds, my Bond-men and Bond-women, and every Soart of trade amongst my own Servants, so that I live in a kind of Independence on every one but Providence. However this Soart of Life is without expense, yet it is attended with a great deal of trouble. I must take care to keep all my people to their Duty, to set all the Springs in motion and to make every one draw his equal Share to carry the Machine forward."

Tidewater plantations were worlds of their own. Having few roads or towns, most colonists spent their lives at home. Lacking stores, they grew most of their food and made most of their clothes. Unable to travel easily, they took their pleasure at home; neighbors and visitors were few. John Mason described the plantation life of his father, George Mason, who built Gunston Hall in Fairfax County: "It was very much the practice with gentlemen of landed and slave estates . . . to organize them as to have considerable resources within themselves; to employ and pay but few tradesmen, and to buy little or none of the coarse stuffs and materials used by them . . . Thus my father had among his slaves carpenters, coopers, sawyers, blacksmiths, tanners Furriers, shoemakers, spinners, weavers, and knitters, and even a distiller." The planter spent his morning on horseback, conferring with his overseer and observing his slaves. Returning home to his office, he would devote the afternoon to his accounts, computing expenses and profits, ordering supplies, and writing merchants in English and Virginia ports to get the highest prices for his produce. Here also he read the *Virginia Gazette* and books and periodicals from London. But it was not as easy a life as it sounds; as the Reverend James Maury observed in 1762, "And though you suppose them born to the greatest fortunes, yet the prudent management of a large Virginia estate requires so frequent and close an inspection, in order, not only to improve but preserve it, that the possessor, when once he comes to be charged with the care of it, can expect but little of that leisure and repose which are requisite for a pleasurable or successful engagement in such parts of literature as the languages, criticism, and curious and deep researches into antiquity."

The planter's wife was equally busy. A niece of Helen Skipwith Coles, wife of Tucker Coles of Smallwood plantation in Albemarle County, wrote of her: "Aunt Helen . . . was up by sunrise every day, making the rounds of the kitchen, the smokehouse, the dairy, the weaving room, and the garden, with a basket of keys on one arm, and of knitting on the other, whose busy fingers never stopped; and who, as the needles flew, would attend to every one of the domestic duties and give all the orders for the day, only returning to the house in time to preside at a bountiful breakfast table, then resuming her rounds to visit the sick, to give out work to the spinners and weavers, and those engaged in making clothes for the hands; prescribing for all usual ailments of the young and old in the absence of the doctor, caring for her flowers, and then sitting down to her books and her music."

The construction of the great plantation houses was part of the consolidation of dominance by the gentry—a process that by the 1740s inaugurated a stable political authority in Virginia that was exceptional in British America. The Georgian form of the great houses, with their paneled and pilastered walls, parquet floors, molded ceilings, marble fireplaces, and grand staircases, continued to communicate established social values for many years to come. Indeed, although Savannah was taken by the British in 1778, the Southern colonies for the most part avoided the upheavals of the Revolution, and plantation society thrived and prospered for a century more.

opposite page
First-floor passage in Kenmore, Fredericksburg, Virginia. The "Mary Ball Washington Clock," named after George Washington's mother, stands beside the door. Home to the president's sister, Elizabeth, and brother-in-law, Fielding Lewis, Kenmore owes its extraordinary plasterwork to the same French craftsman that worked at Washington's Mount Vernon estate.

The Pitt-Dixon House on Duke of Gloucester Street in Williamsburg, Virginia, is a reconstruction of the house built by George Pitt between 1717 and 1719. His apothecary shop, the Sign of the Rhinoceros, stood behind the house. In 1774 Pitt sold the house to John Dixon, who published the *Virginia Gazette* in the building next door. The original Pitt-Dixon House was destroyed by fire in 1896; it was rebuilt in 1936.

At this end of the seventeenth-century room in the Pitt-Dixon
House, Williamsburg, Virginia, is a court cupboard of oak, pine,
and maple, attributed to the shop of John Taylor of Cambridge,
Massachusetts. Taylor worked as "college joyner" for Harvard
between 1638 and 1682, and during this time he is believed to have
made this and five related cupboards. The maple Cromwellian
chairs were made in New England between 1640 and 1670.

opposite page
This doorway in the Pitt-Dixon House leads from the seventeenth-
century room into the center hall. To the left of the doorway is a
brass lantern clock made in London in 1653. The walnut tall-
case clock in the hall was made by Henry Taylor of Philadelphia
about 1740.

The maple armchair in the left foreground of the seventeenth-century room in the Pitt-Dixon House, made in New England about 1660, is drawn up to a late-seventeenth-century English double-gateleg table covered with an Alpujarra carpet. The two books on the table are a bible published in Cambridge, England, in 1673 and *Country Farme*, by Charles and John Stevens, published in London in 1616. The late-seventeenth-century brass chandelier hanging over the table is Dutch or English. Beside the fireplace is an English stump work writing coffer on a New York dropleaf trestle-base table, made about 1700. Over the mantel a breastplate and matching back piece from a suit of armor, attributed to a Milanese armorer of about 1575, are mounted on either side of an Italian cabasset of the same period. The white-oak-and-pine chest of drawers between the windows, made in eastern Massachusetts about 1690, retains traces of its original red paint. Beside the chest is an English beechwood cane chair of about 1690.

The maple-and-chestnut table with turned stretchers against the wall in the parlor of the Pitt-Dixon House was probably made in Massachusetts about 1700. The tabletop is inset with slate cut to conform to its octagonal shape. Behind the tea table is a walnut Spanish-foot easy chair made in Boston about 1710, and between the windows stands a black-walnut dressing table, probably made in Philadelphia about 1710; its curved, crossed stretchers and arched skirt make it a fine early example of the form. The late-seventeenth-century looking glass above it is also from Philadelphia. Another early Pennsylvania piece is the walnut desk on frame in the corner, which was made about 1720. The overmantel portrait of William Ashe is attributed to Sir Peter Lely.

above

The interior of Anthony Hay's Cabinetmaking Shop in Williamsburg shows a working, restored eighteenth-century craftsman's shop. It took two men to work a lathe such as that at the end of the shop—a journeyman or master craftsman wielding the chisels to carve the wood and a muscular apprentice driving the "great wheel."

left

The James Geddy House, Williamsburg, was the eighteenth-century home and workshop of a successful family of artisans. More than gunsmithing went on here, however; an inventory taken after James Geddy's death listed brasswork for guns, a turner's lathe, bullet molds, and gunsmith's, cutler's, and founder's tools. The Geddy Foundry was located behind the house; in the eighteenth century the yard around it would have been littered with piles of coal, mounds of slag, and iron and brass waste.

The Taliaferro-Cole Shop in Williamsburg houses the trades of
harness maker and saddler. Coachmaker Charles Taliaferro
practiced his trade for over thirty years; he purchased this property
in the early 1770s. He also operated a brewery and a warehouse,
hired out boats, and sold foodstuffs and other supplies to outfit
ships at nearby College Landing. The harness maker and saddler
was a busy craftsman since saddles and harness were much in
demand in colonial Virginia. Leather ranked with iron and wood
as one of the most useful raw materials in the eighteenth century;
leather workers also produced leather water buckets, fire hoses,
inkwells, and helmets, among other common goods.

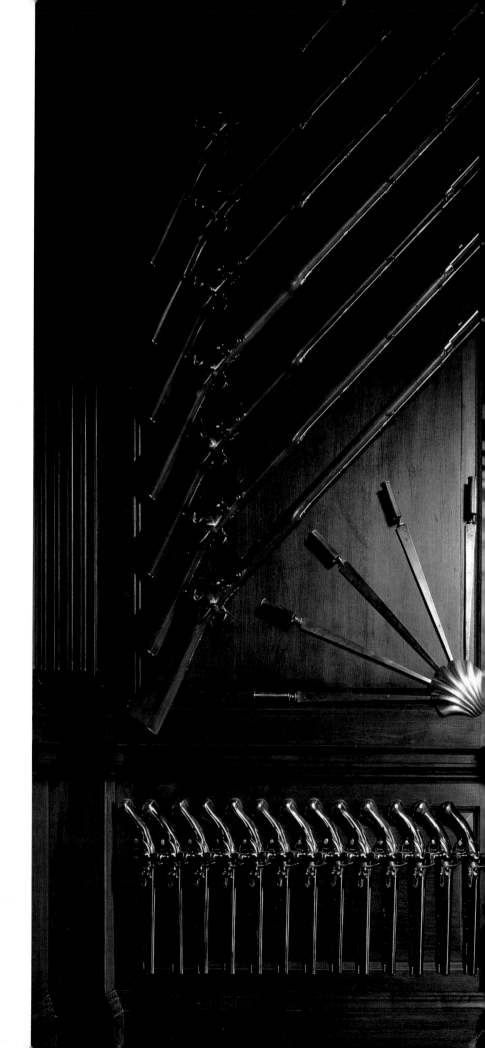

The staircase of the Governor's Palace, Williamsburg, displays an impressive collection of firearms and swords. Like the guard chambers of royal residences in England, the hall of the palace functioned as a screening area where visitors wishing to see the governor were "sorted out." People with particularly important business were escorted upstairs by the butler for an audience with his excellency. Moving through the entry hall and up the wide staircase toward the governor's elegant middle room, visitors were no doubt impressed by the grand procession of spaces and their ornamental displays of arms. The displays served two primary purposes: they were a potent symbol of the crown's power in a region where physical might was not an inconsiderable factor, and they proclaimed the governor to be a gentleman, accustomed to the trappings of regional authority and wealth. Beyond a final set of doors, in the elaborately appointed middle room, the governor himself, amid considerable pomp, received visitors and transacted business in privacy.

226

Lord Botetourt's English butler, William Marshman, had his office in this pantry in the Governor's Palace, Williamsburg, Virginia. From here he managed the household staff of twenty-five servants and slaves. Marshman slept on the bed under the left window in order to secure the contents of this important room, and kept the household accounts at the library table in the foreground. By 1770 Marshman received the highest salary of any member of Governor Botetourt's staff. "No Servant had ever heaped upon him such continual proof of kindness from any Master," wrote Marshman after the governor's death, "as I received from that Generous and Good Man."

Stratford Hall, overlooking the Potomac River in Westmoreland County, Virginia, was built by Thomas Lee about 1738. Lee's massive mansion adapts the baroque monumentality of the English school of Sir John Vanbrugh and Nicholas Hawksmoor to the region's climate, building materials, and social needs. It uses an H-plan, a Jacobean type that had been recently revived in English Georgian houses, but local colonial architecture was just as likely an influence; at the first Virginia capitol, Lee had experienced the generous lighting and ventilation of a large H-plan building. In its two wings, Lee's H-plan provided abundant space for the activities important to his generation of Virginians. The two largest rooms on the upper floor of the garden wing were given to dining and sitting. Four cool bedchambers were located on the ground floor of the more private back wing. Stratford, an original creation, clearly speaks of the high status of its owner, the extent of his hospitality, and to our modern eyes, his vigorous, provincial spirit.

231

This bedchamber at Stratford Hall is known as Mother's Room. The mistress of the house occupied this large bedroom, which was the hub of the plantation; here she gave orders to the servants and here she bore her children. The late-eighteenth-century mahogany bed may have been made in Charleston, South Carolina. The fabric used throughout the room is a reproduction of a *toile de Jouy* of about 1750 depicting America paying homage to France. Robert E. Lee, a descendant of Thomas Lee, slept in the crib in front of the window after his birth on January 19, 1807.

opposite page
The fireplace of the kitchen at Stratford, altered in the last century, has been restored to its original dimensions. Twelve feet wide, six feet high, and five feet deep, it is large enough to roast a whole ox. In the right side wall of the fireplace are baking and warming ovens. The small copper still was used to prepare spirits or medicines.

At the center of the house and on the *piano nobile* is the great hall of Stratford. The hall, 29½ feet square, with a 16½-foot coved ceiling and ornately decorated with Corinthian pilasters, is one of the most handsome rooms created in colonial America. Each of the four large windows has a window seat and folding shutters. Double doors at the north and south open to the outside; those on the east and west lead to wide passages floored with pine boards some thirty feet long. Used only in the summer, the hall has no fireplaces. Beginning about 1720, a thriving market in English architectural handbooks offered a potpourri of classical elements from which a housebuilder could assemble a unique expression of his individual taste and personality. The opulence and grandeur that often resulted not only announced one's enormous economic success but also expressed a desire to bring Virginia, seen as a cultural backwater, into the intellectual mainstream.

235

Wilton, in Richmond, Virginia, was built in 1750–53 for
William Randolph III on a high bluff overlooking the James River,
some fifteen miles from its present site. The original plantation had
two offices, a storehouse, and a dairy and kitchen as outbuildings.
Always a well-known house but frequently neglected, it was
described by one visitor in 1833 as "such ruin: Broken down fences,
a falling piazza, defaced paint, banisters tied up with ropes, etc."
In 1933 the Colonial Dames took title to Wilton, moved it to its
new site, and restored and furnished it. Its exterior has some of the
finest brickwork in the state, while its interior is paneled from floor
to ceiling in every room.

The mahogany kneehole desk in the parlor of the Hennage collection, Williamsburg, Virginia, was made in Newport, Rhode Island, 1755–65. On it is an eight-day shelf clock inscribed "John Crawley/Philadelphia," where one John Crawley worked from 1803 to 1825. The English or American gilded and walnut-veneered looking glass, about 1765, descended in the Frisbee family of New York and northern New Jersey.

The paneling in the dining room of the Hennage collection, Williamsburg, Virginia, comes from Greenspring Manor in New Castle, Delaware, built about 1760 and demolished in 1929, and the marble hearth comes from a mid-nineteenth-century house in Atlanta, Georgia. Set into the paneling is a still-life painting by the American artist Frederick Stone Batcheller. The dining room tables, a pair, were probably made in Boston about 1800. Around them are two sets of New York mahogany chairs, about 1795, that descended in the Riker and Davenport families of New York City. The design of the chair backs is from Thomas Sheraton's *Cabinet-Maker and Upholsterer's Drawing-Book*.

The gilded mahogany looking glass in the parlor of the Hennage collection, Williamsburg, Virginia, was made in England or Philadelphia about 1760. Under it is a Philadelphia mahogany dressing table of 1760–90, which descended in the Varick and Stout families of New York City. The mahogany Philadelphia easy chair by the fireplace dates from the 1770s; it is inscribed "McClenachen" in chalk on the back rail, for the family in which it descended. The mahogany tea table and walnut desk-and-bookcase were also made in Philadelphia, 1760–90, as was the walnut easy chair in the foreground, which dates from about 1760.

An impressionist still life by Anna S. Fisher hangs above the English mantelpiece of about 1750 in the library of the Hennage collection, Williamsburg, Virginia. The mahogany easy chair was made in Boston, about 1760–70, for Timothy Danielson of Brimfield, Massachusetts; the Philadelphia mahogany armchair dates from about 1770. The mahogany card table in front of the window was made in Newburyport, Massachusetts, 1760–80.

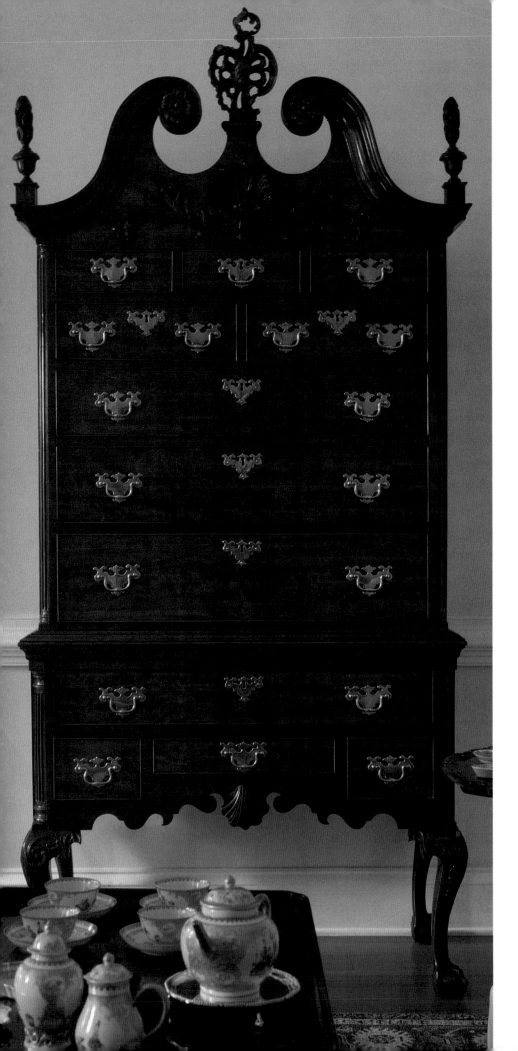

The mahogany and mahogany-veneered high chest of drawers in the parlor of the Hennage collection was made in Philadelphia, 1760–90, and descended from Benjamin Franklin or his daughter, Sarah Franklin Bache, to Henrietta Bache Jaye.

opposite page
Above the Philadelphia mahogany sofa, 1765–85, in the parlor of the Hennage collection, Williamsburg, Virginia, is a set of twelve floral prints, one for each month, printed by Robert Furber and John Boles in London in 1749. The mahogany table in front of the sofa was probably made in Boston, 1755–70, and descended in the Williams and Shoemaker families of Pennsylvania. The mahogany chairs were both made in Philadelphia; the armchair about 1760–90 and the side chair, one of a set of six, about 1770. The gilded mahogany looking glass, made in England or Philadelphia about 1760, is labeled by John Elliott Sr. of Philadelphia. The Philadelphia mahogany dressing table, 1760–90, was formerly in the collection of Reginald Lewis.

Dominating the bedroom of the Hennage collection, Williamsburg, Virginia, is a four-post mahogany bed, made in Charleston, South Carolina, 1790–1800, with reeded, carved, and inlaid posts in the Hepplewhite style. The Chippendale mahogany card table at the foot of the bed, made in Philadelphia about 1760–80, has a gadrooned apron border, molded legs, and is embellished with scrolled brackets.

Thomas Jefferson assisted in the design of Belle Grove Plantation in Middletown, Virginia, which was built in 1794 by Major Isaac Hite Jr., James Madison's brother-in-law. Further help, including aspects of the parlor's carving and interior design, came from *Pain's British Palladio; or, the Building General Assistant* (1786). The native-limestone dwelling, surrounded by the fertile farmland of the northern Shenandoah Valley, was described early in the nineteenth century as "doubtless the most splendid building west of the Blue Ridge." The Charles Peale Polk portraits of Major Isaac Hite Jr. and his mother-in-law, Nelly Conway Madison (James Madison's mother), are two of seven commissioned by Hite in 1799.

opposite page

The Chinese-style dining room of Gunston Hall, Mason Neck, Virginia, was used by the Mason family when they entertained guests. (The Little Parlor served as the family dining room and as George Mason's office and study.) The mantel and overmantel were reconstructed in 1950 based on traces of the original, which had been removed in the nineteenth century. The Chinese export porcelain service on the table was much more costly than the "everyday" salt-glazed tableware stored and used in the family dining room. George Mason, an early Revolutionary thinker, began to build his new house in 1755, about five years after his marriage, and named his home Gunston Hall after an ancestral home in Staffordshire, England. Although Mason applied his own skills in the design of the exterior and floor plan of his new house, he felt the need of an experienced craftsman to complete the interior, and brought William Buckland, an Oxford-born carpenter-joiner, to Virginia from London to complete Gunston Hall.

Kenmore, in Fredericksburg, Virginia, was built by Fielding Lewis in 1752–56. One of the finest of the eighteenth-century plantation houses, the mansion was erected by an unknown builder. The freestanding portico on the riverfront side was the height of mid-eighteenth-century English fashion, and many interior details give evidence of the Lewis's desire to build well and in the then current English styles. The relation between the exterior cornice and the entire facade is more successful at Kenmore than at most houses built in Virginia at that time, and the rooms are well planned and flow easily into one another. In 1750 Fielding Lewis married Elizabeth (known as Betty) Washington, George Washington's sister, and to the marriage Betty brought a substantial dowry of £400 and two female slaves. Lewis soon decided to build a new house for himself and his wife, a house that would reflect the couple's position in the community and be close to his riverfront businesses in Fredericksburg. He chose an 863-acre tract outside the town for its easy access to the Lewis warehouse, ropewalk, and dock on the Rappahannock River, and to his tenements and other properties in Fredericksburg.

The ornate plasterwork and wood carving in the drawing room at Kenmore appear to have been added after the house was finished—possibly as late as 1775. They reflect the styles popularized in England at the time by Robert Adam and his contemporaries. The craftsman who executed the drawing room plasterwork, the most elaborate in the house, is unidentified, but Fielding Lewis referred to him with annoyance as a "Frenchman" when writing in 1775 to his brother-in-law George Washington about the length of time the work was taking. According to

correspondence at Mount Vernon, the same Frenchman also worked on the interior of that house. The overmantel depicts Aesop's fable "The Fox and the Crow"; it is said that Washington suggested this design to keep those living in the house on guard against flatterers. The mahogany chairs are from Massachusetts, 1760–75; the drop-leaf table in the center of the room is an eighteenth-century southern piece. The cut-glass chandelier is English or Irish and dates from about 1760.

preceding pages

The walls of this bedchamber at Kenmore have been repainted the original Pompeian red. The corner sections of the plasterwork ceiling are ornamented with plants that symbolize each of the four seasons—palms for spring, grapes for summer, acorns for autumn, and mistletoe for winter. The side chairs are from Philadelphia, made about 1775. Fielding and Betty Lewis engaged in a variety of economic enterprises, giving them some protection against the vagaries of the tobacco trade, and it appeared that they would lead a quiet and prosperous life at Kenmore. During the 1760s, however, drastic declines in the prices received for tobacco, coupled with import duties imposed by the Townshend Acts, began to create financial problems for Virginians. Pressed by what they saw as unfair and punitive policies, Fielding Lewis and his brother-in-law George Washington gradually turned against the British crown. During the Revolution, Fielding Lewis oversaw Washington's estates as well as his own, and between 1775 and his death in 1781, Lewis financed and helped operate a gun manufactory in Fredericksburg. The war destroyed the economy and currency of Virginia, and Fielding Lewis died embittered and impoverished.

Between about 1757 and his death on December 14, 1799, George Washington guided the evolution of Mount Vernon from a modest farmhouse to what he considered an appropriate setting for his private and public life. Self-sufficiency, agrarianism, and republicanism were fundamental beliefs of Washington and his contemporaries, so it was to the classical design theories of Andrea Palladio that he turned when he began to enlarge Mount Vernon. The major architectural problem Washington faced was the asymmetry of the doors and windows on both the west and the east, or river, facades. About 1759 the roof was raised from one-and-a-half to two-and-a-half stories and the entire house was sheathed with white-pine boards deeply scored with painted rustication to look like blocks of stone. When the two-and-a-half-story house proved to be too small, designs were made in 1773 for additions on the north and south ends of the main block. In 1776 the north addition was raised; it eventually housed the major public room of the house, now called the large dining room. The cupola was built in 1778.

The small dining room at Mount Vernon, Virginia, underwent great changes during Washington's lifetime. The woodwork dates to about 1757–60, while the present carved-wood and plaster ornament was added during a redecoration in 1775, probably at the time the adjacent study was built. In choosing a design for the chimney piece, Washington turned to Abraham Swan's *British Architect*. He employed two extraordinary craftsmen to ensure the faithful replication of the splendid rococo ornament: Bernard Sears as the wood-carver and an unnamed Frenchman for the plaster-work. Washington's estate manager and cousin, Lund Washington, wrote him in November 1775: "The Dining room will I expect be finished this week now come in. It is I think, very pretty. The stucco man agrees the ceiling is a handsomer one than any of Colonel Lewis' although not half the work in it." The French "stucco man" was also working for Fielding Lewis, Washington's brother-in-law, at Kenmore in Fredericksburg, Virginia.

259

George Washington's study at Mount Vernon, more than any other room in the house, reflects the discipline, habits, and practical tastes of its creator. As the principal room on the main floor of the south wing, it was designed for privacy and conference. Martha Washington's grandson, George Washington Parke Custis, who was raised at Mount Vernon, described the room as "a place where none entered" except by direct order. One of the privileged few was Samuel Powel of Philadelphia, who during a visit in 1787 noted that Washington had "a very handsome Study," and remarked on its privacy in a house where "perpetual and elegant hospitality . . . is absolutely requisite." In 1774 Washington supervised most of the construction of the two-and-a-half-story addition to the south end of his house, situating his study just below the principal bedroom, to which it was connected by a simple back stair. The study has Washington's Windsor fan chair, a nineteenth-century cast of Houdon's bust of him over the door, and to the right of the door a plaster bas-relief of Washington done about 1784 by Joseph Wright. The secretary desk was made by John Aitkin in Philadelphia in 1797, and the swivel-seated desk chair by Thomas Burling in New York City in 1790.

Stone was such an unusual building material in Richmond, Virginia, that this building was known as "The Stone House" even in the eighteenth century. The oldest dwelling still standing in Richmond, the house, built before 1783, may have existed before the town was founded. It is now maintained by the Edgar Allan Poe Foundation as a museum of books and mementos relating to the poet, who lived and worked in Richmond. Although there is no known historical association between Poe and this house, he was editor of the *Southern Literary Messenger,* which had offices a few blocks west on Main Street.

The Adam Thoroughgood House in Virginia Beach, Princess Anne County, Virginia, built 1685–1770, is a brick variation of the post-hole "Virginia house" developed by the new gentry. It shares the hall-parlor plan, steep gable roof, and asymmetrical arrangement of openings believed to be characteristic of the post-hole buildings. It also resembles the masonry cottages with gable-end chimneys of western and upland England that must have been a direct influence for some Virginia builders. Unlike the other types tried after the mid-seventeenth-century, this form remained popular both on the plantation and in the city through the end of the colonial era. It was refined in the eighteenth century with more careful proportioning in the size and spacing of windows and with rich, classical detailing, particularly modillioned cornices and sash windows.

opposite page
Although the exterior of the Adam Thoroughgood house is identified by the Gothic verticality of the ends, the interior seems low and horizontal. In its simple and awkward way, the house displays the same mixture of medieval and classical elements that characterized both English architecture and life in the late sixteenth and early seventeenth centuries.

opposite page

Tryon Palace in New Bern, North Carolina, designed by John Hawks for William Tryon, built 1767–70, was partially destroyed by fire in 1798 and rebuilt from 1952 to 1959. Tryon became governor in 1765, and the following year he convinced the assembly to designate New Bern as the capital of the colony by virtue of its central location, and to appropriate funds to build a proper governor's residence. In early 1767 Tryon signed articles of agreement with the English-trained architect John Hawks, who had come to North Carolina with Tryon in 1764, to design and construct a building that would serve as both the governor's residence and the meeting place for the governor's council. The palace—an imposing two-story block with flanking dependencies joined by colonnades—was opened with great ceremony on December 5, 1770.

The council chamber, the largest room in Tryon Palace, was also used to entertain large groups. The eighteenth-century Siena marble mantel was found in England and roughly fits the description of the original, which was destroyed in the fire of 1798. The coat of arms of King George III is displayed in the overmantel and a full-length portrait of him hangs at the left of the fireplace. The English tall-case clock of 1720–30 is made of mahogany and amboina wood; its face is engraved with the name Charles Clay of London. The mahogany council tables with stop-fluted legs are attributed to the Townsend-Goddard shops in Newport, Rhode Island, 1760–70. The eight English Gothic mahogany armchairs of about 1770 are from a set of a dozen; four were possibly made in the shop of Thomas Chippendale. The tall walnut armchair at the left of the table is English, about 1745.

The first-floor dining room of Tryon Palace faces south onto the Trent River and may have been used as an entrance to the palace by those arriving by water. On the English mahogany dining table of about 1770 are a silver epergne made by William Cripps in London in 1751 and four silver candlesticks made by William Ward in Dublin in 1770. Around the table is a set of six mahogany chairs, 1760–70, possibly Irish, and above it is an Anglo-Irish cut-glass chandelier made about 1740–60. The English carpet, probably made at Axminster or Moorfields, dates from around 1770. Above the mantel is a portrait of Mary, Queen of Scots, by an unknown English artist, about 1700–1740. The Philadelphia mahogany tall-case clock case of about 1765 has a dial inscribed with the name of James Warned of London. The English looking glass dates from around 1700.

opposite page

In this view of the first-floor parlor of Tryon Palace, the Soho tapestry chairs have been slipcovered for summer. An eighteenth-century French violin rests on an English mahogany stool of about 1775, and a Worcester tea service of around 1770 adorns the English mahogany tea table of 1760–70. The carved eighteenth-century marble mantelpiece was purchased from Coldbrook Park, Monmouthshire, England. The overmantel painting, *Landscape with Huntsman*, 1639, is by Claude Lorrain.

The mahogany chest of drawers in a second-floor bedroom of Tryon Palace is English, about 1780. The top drawer is elaborately fitted with lidded compartments, pockets, and a mirror on an adjustable strut. The small purse at the right is English, about 1640. It is worked in silver and gold threads on red silk and canvas and is believed to have once belonged to King Charles I. On top of the chest is a pair of Bow porcelain figures of around 1765 depicting Mars and Cupid and Venus and Cupid. In the center is an English embroidery-covered box, about 1750. The pincushion is dated 1741 and bears the initials "M.W." The card case is English, about 1670, and has an embroidered cover.

The English mahogany sofa in the upstairs supper room of Tryon Palace, New Bern, North Carolina, was made about 1760 and is upholstered in canvaswork and trimmed with silk edging, which dates from after 1830. The English Chippendale side chair dates from about the same period as the sofa. The Chippendale-period square-topped tea urn stand on trifid cabriole legs has an elaborately carved pierced gallery in the Gothic style.

The walnut spinet in the first-floor parlor of Tryon Palace was made in 1720 by Thomas Hitchcock in London. The walnut chairs with Soho tapestry covers are from a set of six side chairs and one armchair made for the Earl of Shaftesbury about 1735. The mahogany card table under the English looking glass of around 1770 is attributed to William Vile, London, about 1760. From the same period is the English mahogany tea table with a piecrust top in the corner. The portrait depicts Philip Bowes Broke and is attributed to Thomas Gainsborough, around 1758; below it is an English mahogany card table, 1760–70. The English mahogany side chair next to it is one of a pair, about 1770.

The handsome carved pine mantelpiece in the southwest bedroom on the second floor of Tryon Palace is from Kirby Mallory, Leicestershire, England, and dates from the eighteenth century. Above it is *River Scene*, painted in 1778 by William Ashford. At the foot of the English mahogany tall-post bed of about 1760 is a pair of carved mahogany stools with woven flame-stitch upholstery. The mahogany easy chair at the left is English, about 1750, and two English Queen Anne walnut side chairs of 1720–40, from a set of six, flank an English mahogany card table of about 1740. The Persian carpet dates from the seventeenth or eighteenth century.

The Governor's Bedroom on the second floor of Tryon Palace contains a handsome English mahogany bed of about 1760 with elaborately carved posts, applied brackets, and hairy-paw feet. A bonnet-topped Massachusetts Queen Anne high chest of drawers of burl walnut with gilded shells, about 1740, dominates the far wall. One of a pair of English or Dutch walnut torchères, 1690–1700, stands to the right of the high chest. The overmantel seascape is Dutch, about 1750. The mahogany night table with chamber pot cupboard in the foreground is English, about 1770; the brass double candlestick on it dates from 1750–70 and is also English. The Turkish prayer rug was made in the last half of the eighteenth century. Refurnishing the second floor of the palace was aided by the Hawks floor plan, which designated where each bed was to be placed.

The library on the first floor of Tryon Palace contains copies of most of the books listed in the inventory of Governor William Tryon's Fort George, New York, house. The overmantel painting, school of Jan Peeters, dates from 1720–40. The English mahogany armchair of 1760–70 reflects the then current Chinese influence. The walnut Queen Anne side chairs of 1715–25 are from a set of four. The mahogany kneehole desk of about 1760 and the folding stepladder of about 1780 are both English, as is the early-eighteenth-century brass chandelier. The armorial carpet is Spanish. During the restoration of the palace it was discovered that the architectural drawings by John Hawks were known to have been in the possession of Hawks's grandson, the Reverend Francis Lister Hawks, as late as the 1850s. His papers were traced to the New-York Historical Society in New York City, where the plans were found. An additional set of plans, believed to be the final, or contract, set, was later discovered in the British Public Records Office in London.

Afterword

BETWEEN 1600 AND 1789 the raw American wilderness became a burgeoning nation. Relying on their indigenous economic strengths, the thirteen British colonies prospered beyond many settler's greatest dreams. Trade, timber, and culture dominated New England; the Middle Colonies became the "bread basket" of British America; and the southern colonies bloomed into a plantation-based tobacco and rice aristocracy. As these distinct economies were built, so were societies, societies that took shape around the great houses and civic buildings the colonists hoped would be enduring reminders of their wealth, status, and learning.

The differences among the colonies were far less important than the similarities that made American culture different from that of England and Europe. America was and had always been fundamentally different from the mother country. At mid-century the thirteen colonies were approaching maturity and asserting themselves with enormous vigor, clarity, and self-assurance. That maturity crystallized in the self-conscious national self-realization that flowered in the fifties and sixties— a growing sense of the potential power and grandeur of the America of the future. Expansionists began to look west and to formulate the idea of Manifest Destiny that would dominate the continent.

After generations of intellectual and emotional devotion to both provincial government and the mother country, there appeared a new loyalty that stood somewhere between the two, loyalty to America. Before 1776, this was not a nationalism of independence, but a feeling that expected to find self-expression within the framework of the British Empire. Conflicts of economic interest and political ideologies alone did not necessarily and inevitably produce civil war; nor, indeed, did conflict in religion, or in culture, or even politics. All these things might have been adjusted peaceably. But when pride was pitted against pride, when the ideal of American liberty confronted the ideal of imperial unity imposed by force, civil war became, in the nature of men and things, inevitable. Given the men, their convictions, and their mood—given, that is, the self-consciousness and the self-confidence of the American mind—the outcome could hardly have been otherwise.

Americans had passed through an intellectual revolution and created a new culture. A new nation was brought forth, the keynote of whose thought and literature, to be heard above all others, was liberty, the principle of freedom. For John Adams, 1776 ushered in a "new World, a young World, a World of countless Millions all in the fair Bloom of Piety."

Illustration Credits